# Simple

# Desserts

# Simple Desserts

# Ken Haedrich

BANTAM BOOKS
New York   Toronto
London   Sydney   Auckland

SIMPLE DESSERTS
A Bantam Book / October 1995

Copyright © 1995 by Ken Haedrich.
COVER AND INTERIOR ART BY KRISTIN HURLIN

BOOK DESIGN BY ELLEN CIPRIANO

Library of Congress Cataloging-in-Publication Data
Haedrich, Ken, 1954–
Simple desserts / Ken Haedrich.
        p.    cm.
Includes index.
ISBN 0-553-37453-2
1. Desserts.    I. Title.
TX773.H22    1995
641.8'6—dc20                                    95-4452
                                                CIP

*Published simultaneously in the United States and Canada*

Bantam Books are published by Bantam Books, a divi-
sion of Bantam Doubleday Dell Publishing Group, Inc.
Its trademark, consisting of the words "Bantam Books"
and the portrayal of a rooster, is Registered in U.S.
Patent and Trademark Office and in other countries.
Marca Registrada. Bantam Books, 1540 Broadway,
New York, New York 10036.

PRINTED IN THE UNITED STATES OF AMERICA
FFG   10 9 8 7 6 5 4 3 2 1

*A lot of very fine folks will go through life
never having a book dedicated to them.
Given the current state of world affairs, worse
fates could befall you. On the other hand,
you—who buy my cookbooks and allow me
to do what I love most: sharing good recipes,
ideas, and experiences—deserve to be duly
recognized. So I dedicate this book to you,
my reader, with gratitude.*

# Contents

# Acknowledgments

I'd like to thank my many friends and colleagues who, by their encouragement, support, advice, and assorted kindnesses, helped make this book possible, and the past year one I will always fondly remember.

At Bantam, my editor Fran McCullough continues to shepherd my manuscripts through the editorial gauntlet with a caring hand. Thank you, Fran. And many more thanks to the rest of the Bantam team, including Nita Taublib, Susan Corcoran, Barb Burg, Lauren Janis, Chris Tanigawa, and Maureen Cosgrove; you're all an absolute pleasure to work with. Also in New York, my agent Meg Ruley gets another great big hug for her always-cheerful, uplifting phone calls.

In Chicago, Lisa Piasecki deserves more appreciation than I could ever express here. Same goes for Brenda McDowell. You gals are wonderful. A special thanks to Paul Tutt for his support. To Joan McGrath and Myrna Pedersen, you are the best at what you do.

In Michigan, Kristin Hurlin is the incredibly gifted artist who did the cover illustration for this and my previous books. Thanks for gracing my books with your beautiful work.

In California, my gratitude to John Carroll, a gracious host, fellow writer, and overall fine person.

Back home, I'm grateful for the generosity of Scott and Patti Biederman, and Steve and Jan Panagoulis; I wish all of you the prosperity you deserve.

Chef Jeffrey Paige of the Canterbury Shaker Village is one of the hardest-working nice guys I know, but never too busy to take one of my calls. Thanks, Jeff!

My neighbor, Elzey Burkham, will no doubt cry for joy from the top of nearby Stinson Mountain when I finally get a fax machine of my own. Until then, he continues to be as graceful about my intrusions as a fellow could possibly be. You're a saint, Elz.

To my children, Ben, Tess, Ali, and Sam: I apologize for the many days when there was nothing to eat at dinnertime other than four variations of Mocha Brownie

Cheesecake, some not even very good. You were all very understanding, and I am eternally grateful, not to mention slightly overweight.

To KP, love of my life, head sparring partner, co-pilot, main squeeze, and incurable beach potato: I look forward to every new day with you.

Finally, to my parents and siblings, I always appreciate your love and support; thanks for being there when I need you.

# Simple Desserts

# Introduction

A couple of years ago, I was listening to a radio guru who asked: If you knew you had only a very short time to live, how would you change your life? I went trolling around in the depths of my soul to see what I might find. There were no big surprises, really. I'd spend more time with Karen and the kids. Read more. Floss less. Learn to play the piano better. Swim, ski, or hike every day. And—oh, yes—eat a lot more dessert!

I took the message right to heart and began work on this book of desserts. At the same time, I began to wonder: Why is it that we keep desserts at arm's length? Why don't we allow ourselves to enjoy desserts more regularly, and take them as seriously as the rest of our cuisine? Given the current climate of health consciousness, abstention, and "lite" eating, an unabashed dessert eater today is considered almost dysfunctional.

Certainly, the language we use to describe desserts has not helped. We tag chocolate, tortes, tarts, pies, and anything else slightly sweet, rich, or pleasurable with adjectives right out of the devil's lexicon. They're sinful, decadent, seductive, sensual, or sexy. We have a *weakness* for cheesecake, we're *addicted* to chocolate, *hooked* on white chocolate mousse with strawberries. On the other hand, beans, grains, greens, vegetables, and fish are wholesome, virtuous, and good for you. Nobody says they're addicted to steamed kale (though I happen to be). I use these terms myself sometimes, but I think we should learn to ignore their negative implications.

So when I speak about simple desserts, I'm not just talking about simple to prepare, though that is certainly a part of it—and I'll get to that in a minute. I'm also talking about a simpler approach to dessert, one that's more celebratory and capable of being integrated into everyday eating. We must remember that dessert—be it a lustrous bowl of ripe fruit in season, or a sliver of rich cheesecake—is just another course, one we should savor without guilt or undue significance. A sweet little something balances an otherwise savory repast. There's nothing wrong with even a rich dessert now and then if we don't overdo it. And there are many less rich, moderately sweet desserts we can enjoy on a regular basis.

So what *is* a simple dessert? A simple dessert doesn't take all day to prepare; it satisfies without being overly involved. I love to cook, but when I see a dessert recipe with a crust, filling, topping, icing, two sauces, and buttercream roses pumped out of a pastry bag I run the other way.

Simple desserts require no more skills than you already have; if you can sauté an onion, you can sauté apple slices and cover them with a warm caramel sauce. If you can boil pasta, you can poach pears in wine. I think the reason a lot of cooks stay away from desserts is the silly notion that dessert making requires advanced techniques, a cooking-school diploma, or the cook's equivalent of a green thumb ("What—me, make a dessert? Why, I have recessive baking genes! Can't do it.") But you can do it. Anybody can make a simple dessert, and often with stunning results on the very first try. There are seasonal lessons to learn (how to coax the most out of a pint of sour cherries), visual and tactile clues to success (that center-wobbly stage when a custard is perfectly baked). But these are things you can pick up easily, and they don't require a deft hand—just the willingness to experiment.

Finally, a simple dessert often has a flexible nature. By that I mean a simple dessert should not be so rigid that it can't be adapted to your needs as the situation requires. For instance, if you like custards but sometimes find them too rich, you can easily make them with milk instead of cream. I've alerted you to that in the section on custard, in hopes you'll make them more often. In the section on fruit desserts, besides offering you some of my favorites in that category I've given you guidelines for making fruit soups, with several other yogurt-based variations. My intention in providing you with this supplemental information—alternatives, little tips, and guidelines—is to demonstrate how easy it is to enhance a single idea, or adapt it. I also want to alert you to little things that might trip you up, or make life easier—like how to make perfect pie pastry, for instance.

You will find here a repertoire of recipes covering the desserts I love most. There are pies and tarts, simple cakes, and the slightly more sophisticated tortes. Fruit is often the perfect ending to the perfect meal, and I have mined the possibilities of seasonal desserts in depth. I am incredibly fond of sweet creamy custards and cheesecakes, so there are a good many of each here. Not to mention dessert crepes, cookies, puddings, crisps, cobblers, and a lot of ice creams, sorbets, and other frozen desserts. Some choices, clearly, are richer than others. Fine; that is as it should be. As Julia Child says, we should put these on an imaginary shelf labeled INDULGENCES, where we keep the best butter, gooey chocolate cakes, and all those lovely items—as Julia puts it—that demand "disciplined rationing." Then there are others as uncomplicated and light as a compote of red summer fruit doused with champagne, a little treat I might enjoy every day during the height of the strawberry season.

Much as I believe we all need to eat responsibly, according to our individual needs, I don't hold much faith in contrived low-fat dessert recipes. Many good desserts are naturally low in calories—how many calories do you have to worry about with a bowl of fruit compote, a cookie or two, or a fruit crisp sweetened with a judicious hand? Low-fat recipes are often written only at the expense of flavor and excitement, and often become an exercise in the absurd, if not the impossible (have you ever tried rolling a pie pastry made with oil instead of butter?). If we gradually tailor our tastes to a cuisine designed by nutritionists, where prune whip passes for butter, and skim condensed milk equals real cream, what will we have accomplished? A little moderation is far more effective than a library full of diet books.

Enjoy!

# Bite-Size Beauties: Cookies, Bars, and a Cheesecake Tartlet

Cookies are, without a doubt, the one sweet treat Americans bake more than any other, perhaps even more than all the other treats combined. And why not? They aren't fussy, as cakes can be. They're not yeasted like bread and you don't have to knead them. Unlike pies and tarts, they don't generally have a crust to roll. All you need is a bowl, baking sheet, and an oven. Best of all, they're quick, often into the oven and out in less than half an hour.

Cookies come in an assortment of personalities, making them an ideal choice for dessert. They can be plain or fancy, big and chunky or small and delicate. Some go nicely with other sweets, while others are a dessert unto themselves.

Because we tend to snack on them throughout the day, we seem to have gotten out of the habit of serving cookies for dessert. But a good, simple homemade cookie—especially with the right coffee or tea—is no less noble or satisfying than a piece of cake or pie, and we can dignify them by taking the time to arrange cookies attractively on a dessert tray or platter, rather than letting everybody go after the cookie jar in one big free-for-all.

If you have children, I probably don't have to tell you much about making cookies because you're already a pro. From the time my kids were about two years old, all of them have loved to bake cookies. I like to let them join in because compared to many of the other things I cook or bake, cookie making is relatively uninvolved and safe; you aren't working near the stovetop, and instead of using an electric mixer—a potentially dangerous piece of equipment when little kids are around—you can often get by just creaming your ingredients with a wooden spoon.

A couple of cookie-making tips before you dig into this section to find something that looks good:

> —Always use unsalted butter, as specified. The flavor is superior to and much fresher than salted; the proof is in the finished product.

—Burned bottoms on cookies are a common problem. If that happens to you, double-pan your baking sheet by stacking two like baking sheets together with coins in between them to create an air space buffer. Or, better yet, buy one of the new cushion-air-type sheets with the built-in air space. Bake cookies one sheet at a time, on the center rack, if your oven is small. Or rotate the sheets from the upper to lower shelf midway through the baking, if you're baking more than one sheet at a time.

—Get a big cooling rack, and hang it in a handy location. Plan on doubling the recipe, especially if you're baking with kids. It's amazing how much dough never even makes it into the oven!

# Pecan Apple Butter Thumbprints

*Makes about 2 dozen cookies*

These are so addictive, you'll be sorry I ever gave you the recipe. Those of little willpower, proceed with caution. In fact, the only thing I can say about these that's even slightly negative is that they don't ship well: Because the apple butter is so soft, you can't really wrap them. All the more reason to eat them all yourself. I like to use wheat germ in my baking, for the nutty flavor and nubby texture it adds, and this is one of the best uses I've found for it.

$1/2$ cup (1 stick) unsalted butter, softened
1 egg yolk
$1/2$ teaspoon vanilla extract
1 cup whole pecans, untoasted
$1/2$ cup sugar
1 cup unbleached all-purpose flour
$1/2$ cup plain toasted wheat germ
$1/4$ teaspoon salt
$1/3$ cup apple butter (see Note)

Preheat the oven to 350° and get out 2 large baking sheets.

In a large mixing bowl, cream the butter, egg yolk, and vanilla with a wooden spoon. Set aside. Put the pecans and sugar in the bowl of a food processor and process until finely ground. Add the flour, wheat germ, and salt and process for 5 more seconds. Stir the dry ingredients into the creamed mixture, about one-third at a time, until evenly blended.

Using your hands, roll balls of dough about $1^1/4$ inches in diameter. Place them about 2 inches apart on the ungreased baking sheets, making a deep impression in each cookie with your thumb. If the edges crack a little, don't worry; just push them back together with your fingers.

Bake for 20 minutes, until lightly browned. As soon as the cookies come out of the oven, gently press the end of a wooden spoon into each depression to enlarge it slightly (they will close up a little as the cookies bake). Cool the cookies on the sheet for 3 to 4 minutes, then carefully transfer them to a rack to cool. Store in an airtight container until you're ready to serve. Just before serving, spoon enough apple butter into each depression to fill it. Arrange on a plate and serve.

*Note:* Instead of apple butter, you can use apple cider jelly. Find it at your local health food store, or use the source on page 23.

# Whole Wheat Walnut Refrigerator Cookies

*Makes about 3 dozen cookies*

This is a basic refrigerator cookie, enhanced with two personal touches: some whole wheat flour and walnuts, which gives them an earthy and wholesome profile. You can make these any time of year, but you certainly *don't* want to be without several rolls in the fridge on full alert, come holiday time. Then, on the shortest notice you can whip these out, slice, and bake off a trayful in a heartbeat.

$^1/2$ cup (1 stick) unsalted butter, at room temperature
1 cup plus 2 tablespoons sugar
1 large egg
1 teaspoon vanilla extract
$^3/4$ cup unbleached all-purpose flour
$^3/4$ cup whole wheat flour
1 teaspoon baking powder
$^1/4$ teaspoon salt
$^3/4$ cup untoasted walnuts (see Note)

Using an electric mixer, in a bowl, cream the butter, gradually adding 1 cup of the sugar. Blend in the egg and vanilla extract. Sift the flours, baking powder, and salt. Stir the dry ingredients into the creamed mixture about one-third at a time, until uniformly blended. Set the dough aside.

Put the walnuts and remaining 2 tablespoons of sugar in the bowl of a food processor and finely chop the nuts; keep them a little coarse, not mealy. Tear off 2 sheets of wax paper about 12 inches long and place them on your work surface. Spread half of the chopped nuts over each piece of paper.

Divide the dough in half. Shape each half into a rough ball and place one-half on each piece of paper. Roll each one up in the paper into a cylinder about 1¾ inches thick, coating with the walnuts. Pinch the ends of the paper to seal, then slide the rolls onto a small baking sheet. Refrigerate for at least 3 hours. At this point you can either slice and bake the cookies, or slide the cylinders into a plastic bag for longer storage. The dough will keep well in the refrigerator for about a week, or in the freezer for a month.

To bake the cookies, preheat the oven to 375°. Remove the dough from the paper and slice—with a sharp, serrated knife—about ¼ to ⅓ inch thick; use a sawing motion. Place the cookies on an ungreased baking sheet and bake for 8 to 10 minutes, just until the edges start to brown. Cool briefly on the sheet, then transfer the cookies to a rack to finish cooling. Store in an airtight container.

*Note:* If the dough has been frozen, let it sit at room temperature for 10 to 15 minutes before slicing if it seems too hard. If you'd rather, you can simply work the nuts into the dough instead of coating the outside with them. In this case, chop them coarsely by hand and eliminate the extra 2 tablespoons of sugar.

# New Hampshire Amaretti

*Makes about 3 dozen amaretti*

I call these amaretti, since they're made in the tradition of those Italian almond cookies, though they're not especially true to tradition in several ways. For one, I don't use the intensely flavored bitter almonds of authentic Amaretti; blanched store-bought almonds will do fine, and I use almond extract to deepen the almond flavor. I also use baking powder, which isn't traditional, to give the cookies an almost lacy, open texture. Authentic or not, they're still excellent, alone or with coffee, and especially nice with ice creams, custards, semifreddi, fruit desserts, and fruit sorbets.

3 cups blanched whole almonds (see Note)
1 cup granulated sugar
$1/2$ cup packed light brown sugar
finely grated zest of 1 orange
finely grated zest of 1 lemon
1 teaspoon baking powder
pinch of salt
3 egg whites
1 teaspoon almond extract

Put half of the almonds into a food processor with the cup of sugar and grind to a fine meal; don't overgrind or you'll end up with almond butter. Transfer to a mixing bowl. Put the remaining almonds in the food processor with the brown sugar and grind to a fine meal. Combine with the other ground almonds. Mix in the grated zests, baking powder, and salt.

In a separate bowl, whisk the egg whites and almond extract until frothy, then add it to the ground nut mixture. Mix the dough thoroughly, then set it aside for 15 minutes. Preheat the oven to 325°. Butter 2 large baking sheets.

Using your hands, form balls of dough about 1 inch in diameter and lay them on the sheet, leaving a couple of inches between them; you can also use a spoon and push the dough off it, if you'd rather.

Bake for approximately 20 minutes, until the cookies are golden brown. Cool the cookies on the sheets for 1 minute, then transfer them to a cooling rack. Cool to room temperature, then store in an airtight container. These keep very well.

*Note:* To save time and hassle, don't bother blanching your own almonds. It's so much simpler just to pick up blanched almonds in the baking section of your supermarket.

# The Greenery's Oatmeal Chocolate Chip Cookies

*Makes 2 dozen large cookies*

The Greenery in Rockport, Massachusetts, is one of our family's favorite restaurants on Cape Ann. The food is dependably good, and the bakery case has an enticing selection of cookies, muffins, and pies. Here's one cookie we often buy on our way out to the beach or to nibble as we stroll through downtown. They're sweet and chewy, full of walnuts and chocolate chips. The Greenery makes them big, the size of a saucer; for a dessert tray, make them half the size. And here's a good idea: If you like ice cream sandwiches, these are just the cookies to make them with (see box on page 14).

1 cup (2 sticks) unsalted butter, at room temperature
1 cup packed light brown sugar
1 cup granulated sugar
2 large eggs, at room temperature
1 teaspoon vanilla extract
2 cups unbleached all-purpose flour
1 teaspoon baking powder
1 teaspoon baking soda
$^1/_2$ teaspoon salt
$2^1/_2$ cups rolled oats (not instant)
1 cup chocolate chips
1 cup chopped walnuts, preferably toasted (page 20)

In a bowl, cream the butter, gradually adding the sugars, eggs, and vanilla extract.

In a separate bowl, mix the flour, baking powder, baking soda, and salt. Stir the dry ingredients into the creamed mixture, until uniformly blended. Stir in the oats, chocolate chips, and walnuts. Cover the dough and refrigerate for at least 2 hours, or up to 2 days.

When you're ready to bake, preheat the oven to 350° and butter 2 large cookie sheets. Using about $^1/_4$ cup per cookie, make balls of dough roughly 2 inches in diameter and lay them on the sheet; put only 6 on a sheet, leaving plenty of room for them to spread.

Bake the cookies for 20 to 23 minutes, until they're nicely browned and have a uniform texture across the top. If you press one lightly, it may still seem slightly soft to the touch.

Cool the cookies on the sheets for 1 or 2 minutes, then transfer them to a rack and cool to room temperature. Store in an airtight container.

# Greek Honey and Orange Nut Cookies

*Makes about 2 dozen cookies*

These are in the style of the Greek nut cookies known as *finikia,* as I remember them from a wonderful Greek restaurant I used to frequent in New Jersey. The baked cookies, which look like little mummies, are dipped in an orange-honey sauce then dusted with nuts, sugar, and cinnamon. They're all but addictive, and I just love a little plateful with a cup of ginger tea. These are traditionally served during the holidays.

2 cups toasted whole almonds, cooled (page 20)
1³/₄ cups unbleached all-purpose flour
¹/₂ teaspoon baking powder
¹/₄ teaspoon salt
¹/₂ cup (1 stick) unsalted butter, softened to room
    temperature
¹/₂ cup honey, either orange blossom or clover
1 large egg, at room temperature
2 tablespoons orange liqueur
1 teaspoon orange extract
2 tablespoons sugar
1 teaspoon ground cinnamon

HONEY SYRUP

¹/₂ cup honey
¹/₂ cup water
juice of 1 orange

Finely grind 1¹/₄ cups of the almonds in a food processor. In a medium bowl, mix the nuts with the flour, baking powder, and salt. Set aside.

In another bowl, cream the butter and honey. Beat in the egg, then the orange liqueur and orange extract. Stir the dry mixture into the creamed ingredients until uniform. Cover and refrigerate for at least 2 hours or overnight.

While the dough chills, process the remaining nuts, the sugar, and cinnamon to a fine meal and set aside. Put the syrup ingredients in a small saucepan and put them on the stove.

# *And for Good Measure . . .*

Cookbooks and particularly baking books today often include weight measurements for flour and other ingredients. One reason is that many baking books are written by professional bakers, for whom weight measures are the standard; cups are impractical for large-scale baking.

The other reason is this: Even within the realm of home baking, a cup of flour can weigh anywhere from about 3½ to 5½ ounces, depending on the type and how you measure it. A cup of sifted cake flour, for instance, weighs a fair amount more than a cup of whole wheat flour scooped out of the bin.

Much as I like accurate measurements, I don't weigh flour myself in my day-to-day baking. And I don't include weights in my recipes for the simple reason that I don't think one cook in a hundred uses them or owns a scale accurate enough to register precise results. Better, I think, in the interests of practicality and speed, to simply tell you how I measure flour so you can do it the same way.

I use the "spoon and sweep" method. Hold your dry measure cup over your flour bin—and flour should be in a bin, because getting it out of a bag is nothing but a hassle. Using your hand or a large spoon, fluff the flour up a bit, lift it over your cup, and let it fall in. Once the cup is overflowing, sweep it level with a straight edge—in my case, this usually means my finger. A cup of unbleached all-purpose flour—my basic flour—measured this way will generally weigh 4.25 ounces, give or take a tiny bit. And that's close enough.

Once the dough has chilled, preheat the oven to 350° and butter 2 baking sheets. Shape the dough into 1 1/4-inch balls. Rub the balls between your palms, shaping them into slightly tapered cylinders. Place them on the sheets, leaving a couple of inches between them. Bake the cookies for 20 minutes, or until golden brown, then transfer them to a rack.

Bring the syrup ingredients to a boil, then simmer for 5 minutes, stirring occasionally. Remove from the heat. Place a piece of wax paper 16 inches long near your work area and dust it lightly with some of the chopped nut mixture. Place a couple of the cookies at a time in the syrup, tops down. Let them sit in the syrup for 30 seconds, then remove with a slotted spoon and lay them on top of the nuts on the wax paper. Sprinkle the tops with a little of the nut mixture. Repeat for the remaining cookies.

Cool the cookies, then store in an airtight container.

# Almond Biscotti

*Makes about 2 dozen biscotti*

Since the Italians invented them, I suppose they know what they're doing. But every supposedly authentic imported biscotti I've ever eaten has an airy texture I'm not crazy about. These are more to my liking: much more dense, full of ground almonds, and yet still very dry so they're good for dunking in a cup of coffee. I *cannot* keep these around the house because the kids are so crazy about them, and I have similar concerns for you, whether you live with kids or not. Once you've made a batch of these, you'll want to try the good Biscotti Tiramisu on page 90.

2 cups toasted whole almonds, cooled (page 20)
3/4 cup granulated sugar
1 1/2 cups unbleached all-purpose flour
1/2 teaspoon baking powder
1/2 teaspoon salt
1/2 teaspoon ground cinnamon
5 tablespoons cold, unsalted butter, cut into 1/4-inch pieces
2 large eggs
1 teaspoon vanilla extract
confectioners' sugar to roll the dough in

# How to Make an
# Ice Cream Sandwich

The accompanying oatmeal chocolate chip cookies are perfect for building a great ice cream sandwich: They're soft and chewy, but still sturdy enough to do the job. They bake up relatively flat, so you can fit the whole kit and caboodle in your mouth without leaving stretch marks on your lips. Here's how I do it.

Make the cookies as usual, using a little less dough than specified; bake a trial one, then consider the size in relation to a pint of your favorite superpremium ice cream. Ideally, your trial cookie should be about the same size as the bottom of the container. If it's a little bigger, don't worry; if it's a lot bigger, try again. When you get the size down, bake 12 more cookies the same size (celebrate by eating your trial batch).

Now you will need to cut your ice cream into round slabs, which you will do right in the container. To do this right, the ice cream must be quite firm, but not hard as a rock. Decide just how thick you want your ice cream layer to be. Then, using a very sharp serrated knife, saw the ice cream into slabs of the appropriate thickness; half an inch borders on the skimpy side, an inch leaves no question about your generous nature.

Peel off the paper, slap a cookie on either side, and you're in business.

If you'd like to do some advance work on these, cut the ice cream into slabs. Put them on a chilled baking sheet, cover, and freeze until serving. But don't preassemble and freeze them because the cookies will turn rock hard in the freezer.

Preheat the oven to 350° and get out a large baking sheet. Butter it lightly and set aside.

Put the almonds and granulated sugar in a food processor and chop to a fine meal. Transfer to a large bowl. Put the flour, baking powder, salt, and cinnamon in the processor and process for several seconds. Stop the machine, add the butter, then process just long enough to make a fine meal. Add to the bowl with the ground nuts.

Beat the eggs to liquefy them, then stir in the vanilla. Mix the eggs into the dry ingredients by hand, until the dough packs together. Divide the dough in half.

Sift a generous layer of confectioners' sugar over your work area. Roll half of the dough in it, making a 2-inch-thick log. Repeat for the other half, then lay the logs on the greased sheet leaving some room between them. Flatten the logs *slightly* with your hand.

Bake the logs for 35 minutes, or until the surface resists gentle finger pressure, then transfer the sheet to a rack and cool for 10 minutes. Slide the logs off the sheet onto a cutting board. Set the oven to 300°.

Slice the logs on the diagonal about $1/2$ inch thick. Place the slices back on the sheet, standing them on their original bottoms. Bake for 15 to 25 more minutes; they should become dry, but only *slightly* browned. Transfer the biscotti to a rack and cool.

# Triple Chocolate Chip Nut Cookies

*Makes about 3 dozen cookies*

Here's a triple dose of chocolate (unsweetened, cocoa powder, and chips) for those who wouldn't be satisfied with anything less. Use any kind of nut that you like; toasted walnuts and pecans are wonderful, and macadamia nuts make them extra-special. If you're serving these for dessert, shape the cookies, put them right on the sheets, and refrigerate. Then, about half an hour before dessert just pop them into a preheated oven. The cookies will be soft and still slightly warm when you're ready for them.

4 ounces semisweet chocolate
1 cup (2 sticks) unsalted butter, at room temperature
1 cup packed light brown sugar
$1/2$ cup granulated sugar
2 large eggs
1 teaspoon vanilla extract
$2^{1}/_{4}$ cups unbleached all-purpose flour

$^1/_4$ cup unsweetened cocoa powder

1 teaspoon baking soda

$^1/_2$ teaspoon salt

$1^1/_2$ cups coarsely chopped toasted and cooled walnuts,
    pecans, or macadamia nuts (page 20)

1 cup chocolate chips


Melt the chocolate in the top of a double boiler or a bowl set over hot water, stirring occasionally until the chocolate is smooth. Remove from the heat.

In a bowl, cream the butter, gradually adding the sugars. Beat in the eggs one at a time, then the vanilla.

In a separate bowl, sift the flour, cocoa, baking soda, and salt together.

Stir the melted chocolate into the creamed mixture until evenly blended. Fold in the dry ingredients, followed by the nuts and chocolate chips. Cover and refrigerate the dough for 15 minutes. Preheat the oven to 350° and butter 2 large baking sheets.

Roll the dough into balls about $1^1/_2$ inches in diameter and place them on the sheets. Bake the cookies for about 15 minutes (a minute or two longer if you have refrigerated the sheets), until the tops are puffed and very soft to the touch; they'll firm as they cool.

Cool the cookies on the sheet for 5 minutes, then transfer to a rack and finish cooling.


# Coffee Shortbread Cookies

*Makes about 2 dozen cookies*


Shortbread cookies are among my favorites. I love their texture and unassuming character that makes them a natural companion to so many sweets from ice creams to fruit compotes. These cookies are especially good with ice cream. They're delicately flavored with instant coffee, and not too sweet. Try one after they've cooled—if you think they need it, you can always dredge them in confectioners' sugar. If you have a coffee grinder, brush a few of the fine grounds out of it and add them to the dough (with the dry ingredients); those coffee-brown flecks add a classy touch.


$1^1/_2$ tablespoons instant coffee powder

1 tablespoon boiling water

1 cup (2 sticks) unsalted butter, at room temperature
1 teaspoon vanilla extract
1$^1$/$_3$ cups unbleached all-purpose flour
$^2$/$_3$ cup confectioners' sugar, plus extra for dredging
   (optional)
2 tablespoons cornstarch
$^1$/$_4$ teaspoon salt
$^1$/$_8$ teaspoon ground cinnamon

Put the coffee in a small custard cup or ramekin. Pour the boiling water out of the kettle into your measuring spoon, then immediately pour it over the coffee. Stir with a spoon to dissolve the coffee. Cool for 5 minutes.

In a bowl, cream the butter with the vanilla extract. Blend in the dissolved coffee.

In another bowl, sift together the remaining ingredients (except optional confectioners' sugar). Blend the dry mix, about one-third at a time, into the butter until evenly mixed.

Divide the dough in half. Place each half on a sheet of wax paper and shape into cylinders about 11/2 inches in diameter. Wrap them up in the wax paper and refrigerate for at least 2 hours, or up to 2 days. You can also overwrap the dough in a plastic bag and freeze for up to 2 months; thaw overnight in the refrigerator.

When you're ready to bake, preheat the oven to 325°. Using a serrated knife, slice the cookies about 1/4 to 1/3 inch thick and place them on ungreased baking sheets. Bake for 25 minutes, or until the tops feel firm to the touch.

Transfer the cookies to a rack and cool to room temperature. Dredge the cooled cookies in confectioners' sugar if you like. Store in an airtight container.

# Tess's Whole Wheat Ginger Cookies

*Makes about 30 cookies*

My daughter Tess has three requirements for her ginger cookies: They must be a cinch to make, use all whole wheat flour, and be good and crisp. (I agree with her on the first two counts, but I like mine soft; I just bake them less than she does.) These are a snap, and the whole wheat is perfect for this dark, wholesome cookie. Tess makes these—among other times of the year—for Halloween, when the kids love to down them with plenty of fresh cider. I like mine warm, with cold, cold milk. You choose.

$^1/_2$ cup (1 stick) unsalted butter, softened
$^3/_4$ cup packed light brown sugar
$^1/_3$ cup unsulphured molasses
1 large egg
1 teaspoon vanilla extract
2 cups whole wheat flour
1 teaspoon baking soda
2 teaspoons ground ginger
$^1/_2$ teaspoon ground cinnamon
$^1/_4$ teaspoon salt

In a bowl, cream the butter, brown sugar, and molasses until smooth. Beat in the egg and vanilla extract.

In a small bowl, mix the remaining ingredients. Stir half of the dry ingredients into the creamed mixture. Stir in the remaining dry ingredients until the dough is smooth.

Cover and refrigerate the dough for 15 minutes. Meanwhile, preheat the oven to 350° and adjust the rack to the center position. Lightly butter 1 or 2 large baking sheets.

Roll the dough into balls about $1^1/_4$ inches in diameter. Place them on the sheets, about 2 inches apart. Bake one sheet at a time, for about 13 to 16 minutes; when done, the surface will feel soft or semi-soft to the touch. The less time you bake them, the softer the cookies will be. (After 13 minutes the tops will still seem squishy-soft, but they'll firm up some as they cool.) Cool on a rack and store in an airtight container.

# Chocolate-Glazed
# Peanut Butter Blondies

*Makes 9 bars*

Blondies, first cousins to brownies, are generally based on some sort of loose chocolate chip cookie dough. These treats go a step beyond the basic idea with the addition of peanut butter, chopped peanuts, and a chocolate glaze. The glaze is simple, just melted chocolate chips you scatter on top when the bars come out of the oven.

Because of the chocolate, these should be firmed up in the fridge overnight before you cut and handle them. Keep them in the cooler if you're taking them on a summer picnic. This is a good recipe for kids to make because it's virtually foolproof and everything gets spread in one pan. You can just skip the icing, too; blondies are great without it.

$1/2$ cup (1 stick) unsalted butter, softened
1 cup packed light brown sugar
$1/2$ cup smooth natural salted peanut butter
2 large eggs
$1^{1}/_{2}$ teaspoons vanilla extract
1 cup unbleached all-purpose flour
$1/2$ teaspoon baking powder
$1/4$ teaspoon salt
$1/2$ teaspoon ground cinnamon
$1/2$ cup chopped roasted salted peanuts
$1^{1}/_{2}$ cups chocolate chips

Preheat the oven to 350°. Lightly butter an 8- or 9-inch square pan. In a bowl, cream the butter, brown sugar, and peanut butter until smooth. Beat in the eggs, one at a time, then the vanilla.

In a bowl, sift together the flour, baking powder, salt, and cinnamon. Stir the dry ingredients into the creamed mixture along with the peanuts and $1/2$ cup of the chocolate chips. Scrape the batter into the pan and bake for 30 to 40 minutes; the smaller pan will take longer. When done, a tester inserted in the center of the bars will come out clean, except for a little melted chocolate.

Transfer the pan to a rack and immediately scatter the remaining chocolate chips evenly over the top of the bars. Wait about 7 minutes, until the chips are shiny and melted, then spread the chocolate over the bars. Cool to room temperature.

Cover the bars loosely with foil and refrigerate for at least 2 or 3 hours before slicing; overnight is better.

# The Well-Toasted Nut

Now that I've gotten in the habit, I rarely—unless I'm really in a rush—use untoasted nuts anymore. The reason is simple: Toasted nuts just taste better. Richer, fuller, more complex. It's one of those ridiculously easy cooking tasks whose payoff far exceeds the effort involved.

If you aren't an avowed nut toaster, give it a chance. Before you start a recipe, get in the habit of scanning the list of ingredients, as well as the text, to see if toasted nuts are involved. (It's a logical starting point for many recipes, since the nuts usually have to cool before using them; this leaves time for other prep work.)

I toast all of my nuts in a preheated 350° oven for roughly 8 to 12 minutes. Hazelnuts tend to fall on the high side of this range; walnuts, if they're starting at room temperature, on the low side of it. Bear in mind that if your nuts come from the freezer—and that's where you should store them so they stay fresh—they'll take longer to toast.

Spread your nuts out on a dark baking sheet and put them in the oven. Set the timer. Color is one indication they're done; they'll darken a shade or two. But your nose is the best judge when it comes to nuts: As soon as you catch that first toasty whiff emanating from the oven, they're done. Immediately take them out of the oven and dump them onto a plate or counter to stop the cooking.

Nuts should always cool before you chop and use them, for a couple of reasons. Warm nuts will gum up in the food processor; they'll also melt the butter if you incorporate them into a cookie or other butter-rich dough. When finely chopped nuts are called for, it generally means chopping them to a mealish consistency in a food processor, or by hand if necessary. If coarsely chopped nuts are specified, chop them by hand to make bigger chunks.

The only nuts I generally peel are hazelnuts, because of the bitter skin. When the skins have split from the nuts—which may take as much as 12 minutes of toasting—dump the nuts directly onto a tea towel. Fold the towel over, to cover. Wait a minute, then rub the nuts vigorously through the towel. Most of the skins should rub off, but don't worry about the little bits of skin that adhere.

# Mocha Brownies

Brownies aren't difficult to make, but there is a certain precision about the formula: If you start adding too much or too little chocolate, or butter, or making non-traditional substitutions, you can easily find yourself out in left field. These family favorites stray only slightly left of center, but much to their benefit. There's some instant coffee added, which is almost universally applauded; and whole wheat pastry flour, which keeps them somewhat wholesome and enhances the soft, chewy nature of the brownies. If your kids have a hang-up about whole wheat, they'll never suspect it here.

2 tablespoons instant coffee powder
1 tablespoon boiling water
$1/2$ cup (1 stick) unsalted butter
4 ounces semisweet chocolate
$2/3$ cup sugar
1 teaspoon vanilla extract
2 large eggs, lightly beaten
$1/2$ cup unbleached all-purpose flour
$1/2$ cup whole wheat pastry flour
$1/2$ teaspoon baking powder
$1/4$ teaspoon salt

Put the coffee powder in a custard cup or ramkein. Pour the tablespoon of boiling water over it and immediately stir to dissolve the granules. Set aside.

Preheat the oven to 350°. Butter and lightly flour an 8-inch square shallow cake pan.

In a small heavy saucepan, melt the butter over the lowest possible heat, adding the chocolate as the butter melts. Wait for 1 minute, then remove the pan from the heat and set it aside for 5 minutes, to melt the chocolate. Whisk to smooth. Whisk the sugar, dissolved coffee, and vanilla into the chocolate. Whisk in the eggs until smooth.

In a bowl, sift the remaining ingredients together then blend them into the chocolate mixture until smooth. Scrape the batter into the prepared pan and bake for 35 to 45 minutes, until done; a tester, inserted in the center, should come out slightly gooey, and the goo should be quite hot.

Cool the brownies in the pan, on a rack, to room temperature. Cover and refrigerate until firm enough to slice.

# Cider Jelly Walnut Bars

*Makes up to 1 dozen small bars*

Ever since I moved to New Hampshire 15 years ago, one of my favorite special ingredients has been cider jelly—pure apple cider boiled down to the jelly stage. It's a very old New England specialty; occasionally I'll hear of someone who still makes it at home, but for the most part when I see it, it's commercially made. It packs so much apple flavor that a little goes a long way, making it a very valuable baking ingredient. Here's a bar cookie made with cider jelly, one I like to make for my kids in the fall months. The bars are partially sweetened with another native product, maple syrup, and covered with toasted walnuts. I can't tell you how good these are. You'll just have to try them for yourself.

1 recipe Easy Press-In Shortbread Pastry (page 25)

TOPPING

$^1/_3$ cup cider jelly (see Note)
$^1/_3$ cup maple syrup
$^1/_3$ cup packed light brown sugar
$^1/_4$ cup ($^1/_2$ stick) unsalted butter
$1^1/_2$ cups coarsely chopped toasted walnuts, cooled (page 20)

Prepare the pastry, pressing it into the bottom and slightly up the sides of an 8-inch square baking pan. Prebake as directed and cool. Set the oven to 375°.

Combine the jelly, maple syrup, brown sugar, and butter in a medium-size heavy saucepan. Heat slowly at first, to melt the butter, whisking to smooth out the jelly. Increase the heat and bring the mixture to a full boil. Boil the mixture hard for 1 minute, then remove from the heat and stir in the walnuts. Scrape the mixture into the crust and spread evenly. Bake for 15 minutes, until the entire surface is bubbling hot.

Cool the bars in the pan, on a rack, to room temperature. Cover and refrigerate until you're ready to cut and serve them.

*Note:* Cider jelly can be purchased from Mike Phillips, Lost Nation Cider Mill, Groveton, NH 03582. Ask for a current price list.

# Lemon Cheesecake Tartlets

*Makes 1 dozen tartlets*

These are a lot of fun, little cheesecakes made right in a muffin pan. They can be served plain, of course, and they're wonderful just like that. But part of the fun is putting on the finishing touches; you can spread some of your favorite preserves over the top; or cover the tartlets with fresh sliced strawberries brushed with warmed currant jelly; or arrange fresh small raspberries on top. For informal parties, these can be eaten out of hand; for a sit-down dessert, I like a spoonful of fresh sliced fruit on the side. Make the tartlets the day or morning before you serve them.

> 1 recipe Cinnamon Graham Cracker Crust (page 132),
>    modified (see below)
> 1 tablespoon unbleached all-purpose flour
> 1 teaspoon water

### FILLING

> 8 ounces Philadelphia cream cheese, softened
> $^1/_2$ cup sugar
> 1 large egg, at room temperature
> $^1/_4$ cup sour cream
> finely grated zest of 1 lemon
> $^1/_2$ teaspoon lemon extract
> topping of your choice (optional—see Headnote)

Prepare the graham cracker crust, adding the tablespoon of unbleached all-purpose flour to the crumbs. Add the teaspoon of water to the melted butter and mix as usual.

Preheat the oven to 325°. Butter 12 regular-size (not mini or jumbo) muffin cups. Cut 12 strips of wax paper 6 inches long by $^3/_4$ inch wide. Press 1 strip into each cup, neatly tucked into the bottom seams. It should run down the sides and across the bottom, with an even overhang on each side of the cup. (You'll use these strips later to lift the cheesecakes out of the pan.)

Divide the meal evenly between the cups. Start out by putting a heaping tablespoon into each one, then go back and divide up the remainder evenly. Press the meal first into the bottom of each cup, then about halfway up the sides, so that you have a sort of shallow bowl. Refrigerate.

In a bowl, beat the cream cheese and sugar until smooth. Add the egg and beat just until smooth, then blend in the remaining filling ingredients.

Spoon the filling into the muffin cups, dividing it up evenly between them. Bake for 15 to 20 minutes, just until the tartlets are puffed and set; don't overbake. Cool on a rack, in the pan.

When the tartlets have cooled to room temperature, gently pull up on the tabs to loosen them, but only enough to loosen; don't lift them high, or lift them out. Cover the pan with foil and refrigerate for at least 4 hours.

When you're ready to serve them, carefully lift the cheesecakes out of the pan. Serve as is, or decorate the tops as you please.


# Easy Press-In Shortbread Pastry

*Makes enough pastry for*

*a 9-inch pie pan or 8-inch square pan*

Here's a good, reliable press-in crust for all your bar cookies, easily made in a food processor—a great recipe for pastry phobics because you don't even have to touch the dough, other than to press it into the pan. One trick to making tender, easily pressable pastry is not to overprocess it so that the dough balls up and clumps together in a big mass; it should look a *little* clumpy in the processor, but still be somewhat loose and slightly dry. You just spread the crumbs around in the pan and press them in.

> 1¹/₄ cups unbleached all-purpose flour
> ¹/₄ cup sugar
> ¹/₈ teaspoon salt
> 6 tablespoons cold unsalted butter, cut into ¹/₄-inch pieces
> 1 egg yolk
> 1¹/₂ tablespoons cold water

Put the flour, sugar, and salt into the bowl of a food processor and process for 5 seconds. Take the top of the bowl off and scatter the butter over the flour. Re-cover, then process for 10 seconds, breaking the butter into fine bits.

Blend the yolk and cold water in a small bowl. Take the top off the processor

# Searching for Some Good Bars?

A good press-in crust, like the one on page 25, has many uses—and you might want to explore them if you're a lover of bar cookies. For starters, think of a crusted bar cookie as a sort of shallow pie; that's really all it is. You can't use every filling successfully in a bar, but you can do a lot with a little imagination and a fearless spirit.

Cheesecake fillings, for instance, are a perfect example, and I use them all the time to make bars. If you halve the quantities for a typical 9-inch cheesecake, you'll have just about the right amount of filling for an 8-inch square or 9-inch round pan. Bake for 25 to 30 minutes at 350°, until the center is just barely set.

Fresh fruit pie fillings also work well for bars, but again use about half the total amount of filling. However, use just about the full amount of thickening—cornstarch, flour, or tapioca—so the bars are sturdy enough to eat out of hand. And chop the fruit finer than usual, so the bars stay compact when they bake.

### Any Fruit Bar

Dried fruits are my favorite bar filling, and my kids are crazy about them too. So I've developed a formula for making what I call *Any Fruit Bar.* It goes like this:

Start with 2 cups coarsely chopped, pitted dried fruits; it could be dates, dried pears, dried cherries (I've used the last two in combination), figs, prunes, or other. Combine in a small nonreactive saucepan with 1 cup water; $^1/_4$ cup granulated sugar, brown sugar, or honey; and 1 table spoon lemon juice. Bring to a boil, cover, then lower the heat and cook at an active simmer for 10 minutes. Remove from the heat and let stand for 30 minutes.

Meanwhile prepare and partially prebake the press-in crust. Also prepare the crumb topping (below) and refrigerate. Cool the crust on a rack. Leave the oven on.

Transfer the contents of the pan to the bowl of a food processor and process to a smooth puree. Adjust the consistency of the fruit—if necessary—to that of fruit butter by adding water or fruit juice, one tablespoon at a time.

Spread the fruit paste evenly in the cooled crust. Sprinkle the crumb topping over the fruit, and press on it gently, to even the top. Bake in the center of the oven for 30 minutes, then cool the pan on a rack before slicing. They're easiest to slice if you cover the cooled bars and refrigerate overnight. But they taste best if allowed to sit at room temperature for 30 minutes or so.

## CRUMB TOPPING

$1/2$ cup unbleached all-purpose flour
$1/3$ cup rolled oats
$1/3$ cup packed light brown sugar
$1/2$ teaspoon ground cinnamon
pinch of salt
4 tablespoons cold unsalted butter ($1/2$ stick), cut into
　　several pieces

To make the topping, combine all of the ingredients in a bowl and rub them together with your fingers to form clumpy crumbs. Cover and refrigerate until using.

*Note:* This crumb topping is also excellent for pies and crisps.

again, pour the liquid over the flour, and re-cover. Turn the machine on for 6 seconds. Stop, then stir the contents up from the bottom of the bowl with a fork. Process for 6 more seconds. The pastry will still look somewhat dry and separate. Dump the loose pastry right into your pan. Spread the crumbs around then press them firmly down, and slightly up the sides; they should pack right into place. Cover and refrigerate for at least 15 minutes.

To prebake the pastry, bake in a preheated 350° oven for 25 minutes, then cool on a rack.

# All from the Oven:
# Cakes, Crisps, and a Cobbler

Some people think nothing baked should rightfully be called a simple dessert, but I certainly don't. Not only are these poor misguided souls depriving themselves of a lot of good eating, they're also missing out on the unadulterated pleasure of hands-on baking, of working with good ingredients like flour and butter and fresh fruit. This is no small pleasure in a world that's increasingly dominated by fax machines, computers, endless commuting, and other distractions. One of the reasons people turn to baking is the same reason they turn to gardening, because it restores their soul. If you're already a home baker, you know what I mean.

And if you're not, I suspect what's holding you back is at least a mild case of baking jitters; I see it all the time, so I know how you feel. If that's the case, relax, because here you will find an easy agenda of delicious desserts not only for the baking challenged, but for anybody who loves good food. This includes the crustless crisps and a gorgeous plum cobbler, and a variety of simple cakes anyone can make. The main difference between simple and fancy cakes isn't really ingredients; it's decorative flourishes. I've never been one to tackle anything overly elaborate, but that doesn't mean I'll settle for second-rate flavor. Fancy cakes are swell if you can invest the necessary time and patience to cobble up gorgeous creations; frankly, I know I could master the intricacies. But I'm perfectly happy with a limited selection of crowd-pleasing cheesecakes, tortes, shortcakes, and pound cakes that ask little of me and give back much in return.

One area where beginners need to stay honest with cake baking is in pan size. I know it can be tempting to substitute one size pan for another, or one kind of pan for another when you don't have the one specified. I'm not saying this can't be done. But I can tell you that the same cheesecake baked in an 8-inch springform pan will be a very different thing baked in a 10-inch pan. Even in a 9-inch pan you'd have to adjust for the baking time, and make other changes as well, like increasing the amount of crust.

So if you find yourself gravitating toward a particular kind of cake or other dessert with special pan requirements, invest in the right pan. You won't be sorry.

Crisps and cobblers come right to the table in the pan they're baked in. A glass pie pan will do, but they're that much more inviting baked in a pretty ceramic gratin dish or glazed casserole, especially when guests are coming. If you need a gift idea for a baking friend, why not choose a colorful new baking dish for him or her and bake a special crisp in it? It's a double present they won't soon forget.

Spontaneous baking is great fun, but let me put in a word for regular, ritualistic baking. The problem with spontaneous baking is you're at the mercy of your larder; ritualistic baking requires you to plan ahead. A lot of people I know like to make a crisp or cake on the weekend, when their schedule is more flexible, less compressed than during the week, when there's more time to relax and enjoy the fruit of their effort. These folks incorporate that knowledge into their weekly shopping trip, stocking up on butter, brown sugar, apples, pears, or whatever is good and ripe. Try it yourself. Sometimes I like to sit down with a cookbook and browse for a new recipe. I'll read it through, and if it gets me excited I'll jot down any ingredients I need to make it. Set aside a certain time one evening a week to indulge yourself like this. You deserve it.

# Cheesecake

According to surveys, cheesecake is America's favorite dessert. The universally loved version the surveys are based on is what we call New York cheesecake; some call it plain, but I think that hardly does justice to a well-made New York cheesecake—rich and creamy, with just a hint of lemon.

New Yorkers may not recognize the existence of other cheesecakes, but the rest of us know there's a lot of good cheesecake out there beyond the George Washington Bridge. This section includes a couple of shining examples.

Mixing a cheesecake is easiest if you have a freestanding mixer, such as the KitchenAid, which most serious home cooks eventually come to find indispensable. A hand-held mixer will work fine too, but you must be extra-careful not to overbeat the batter. Or mix it by hand; just be sure the batter is smooth. Overbeating tends to incorporate too much air, which may cause the cake to rise and then fall too rapidly, causing the surface to crack as it cools. This is not the end of the world since the defect is primarily visual, and many cheesecakes are covered with a topping anyway. It's just something to watch for.

It is very important that your eggs, cream cheese, and sour cream are at room temperature. Otherwise, the batter won't mix properly which will increase your baking time.

As for the ongoing debate about the importance of using a water bath to cook your cheesecakes in, let me say this: There's strong evidence that a water bath produces a slightly superior cake (more creamy, and slightly better volume). However, my own findings suggest that using low oven heat and a pan of water off to the side in the oven produces results essentially equal to all but the most practiced eye of finicky bakers, people you probably shouldn't invite over for dessert anyway. Sometimes I don't even use the pan of water, or I forget it, and still get wonderful cheesecakes.

# A Great New York Cheesecake

*Makes 10 servings*

I once had a business making cheesecakes for local restaurants, a good way to learn about the cheesecake preferences of the American public. The fact that this New York–style cake was the most popular taught me that most people like a plain cheesecake. On the other hand, the following cake—crowded with brownies, flavored with coffee, and iced with chocolate—was just as popular, which taught me precisely the opposite. So I offer you both. I think most cooks don't do a good job with homemade cheesecake because they fail to observe one simple rule: Keep the temperature down. It is far better to bake a cheesecake longer at a low temperature than to bake it quicker at a higher temperature. I like a creamy cheesecake, so I use sour cream in the custard as opposed to all cream cheese, which gives you a more compact, drier cake. You have to make this at least 24 hours ahead, so the cake has plenty of time to chill and firm before serving. But I think it's even better after 48 hours, so plan accordingly. The sour cream topping is optional, but I find the majority of people prefer it over a naked cake.

> 1 recipe Cinnamon Graham Cracker Crust (page 132)
> 1 pound Philadelphia cream cheese, at room temperature
> $^3/_4$ cup sugar
> 3 large eggs, at room temperature
> 1 cup sour cream
> 1 teaspoon vanilla extract
> $^1/_2$ teaspoon lemon extract, *or* finely grated zest of $^1/_2$
>    lemon

## SOUR CREAM TOPPING (OPTIONAL)

1 cup sour cream
2 tablespoons sugar

Preheat the oven to 350°. Prepare the graham cracker crust and press it into the bottom and up the sides of an 8-inch springform pan. Bake for 10 minutes then cool on a rack. Adjust the oven shelf to the center position and put a shallow pan of hot water off to one side on the shelf. Adjust the heat to 325°.

In a large bowl, beat the cream cheese with an electric mixer, gradually adding the sugar; use the flat beater if your mixer has one. Beat in the eggs on medium speed, one at a time, mixing just until blended after each addition. Gently beat in the sour cream, vanilla extract, and lemon until uniform.

Pour the batter into the crust and bake on the center rack for 60 to 70 minutes. When done, the cake will have risen slightly, especially around the edge, and still appear a little wobbly—though not wet—in the center.

Turn off the heat, open the door of the oven, and let the cake sit undisturbed for 30 minutes. Transfer the cake to a rack to cool. (If you are using the sour cream topping, add it now; see Note). When thoroughly cool, cover and refrigerate for at least 24 hours.

To serve, slice with a warm, sharp knife; rinse and dry the knife after each cut.

*Note:* To make the sour cream topping, combine the sour cream and sugar in a small, nonreactive saucepan. Stir, over very low heat, just until the mixture is somewhat runny and reaches body temperature, about 2 minutes. Pour slowly over the center of the cake, and jiggle the cake so the topping runs up to the edge. Cool for several minutes, then cover and refrigerate.

# *Mocha Brownie Cheesecake*

*Makes 10 to 12 servings*

Whether you're looking to make your mark in the world as a cheesecake magnate, or just looking for something fancy to bring to the neighborhood potluck, this is the dessert you've been waiting for. Once you cut this, you reveal a dark mosaic of brownie pieces surrounded by a creamy coffee-flavored filling. The cake is iced with a thin layer of chocolate ganache, an optional but very classy touch. Truth be told, this is not a snap to make—you must bake a crust and brownies ahead, and make the icing if you're using it—but there's nothing difficult about any of the steps. And you can always use store-bought brownies to eliminate that step. Start this 1 to 2 days before you plan to serve it; an extra 24 hours in the fridge actually improves the texture.

1 recipe Cinnamon Graham Cracker Crust (page 132)
2 cups Mocha Brownies, cut into approximately $^3/_4$-inch squares (page 22)

FILLING

1 pound Philadelphia cream cheese, softened but not too soft
$^2/_3$ cup packed light brown sugar
2 large eggs, at room temperature, plus 1 egg yolk
$^3/_4$ cup sour cream, at room temperature
3 tablespoons coffee liqueur
2 teaspoons cornstarch
1 teaspoon vanilla extract
Chocolate Sour Cream Ganache (page 204—optional)

Preheat the oven to 350°. Prepare the graham cracker crust as directed, but instead of patting into a pie pan, press it into the bottom and most of the way up the sides of an 8-inch springform pan. Bake for 10 minutes in the preheated oven and cool on a rack. Reduce the heat to 325°.

When the crust has cooled, spread the brownie cubes in a single layer in the bottom of the pan.

Using an electric mixer in a bowl, beat the cream cheese and brown sugar on medium speed just until smooth. Beat in the eggs and yolk, one at a time. Blend in the sour cream.

Pour the coffee liqueur into a very small bowl. Add the cornstarch and stir with your finger to break up any clots. With the mixer going, blend the liqueur into the filling along with the vanilla.

Slowly pour the filling over the brownies. Put the cheesecake in the center of the oven and bake it for 50 to 65 minutes. The cake is done when the sides have puffed up, and the center has lost its sheen; it may wobble ever so slightly in the center, but if you're in doubt give it another 7 to 8 minutes. Transfer the cake to a rack and cool to room temperature.

When the cake is thoroughly cooled, cover with foil and refrigerate for at least 24 hours. At some point during the second day, several hours before you plan to serve it, ice the cake with a thickish layer (up to $^1/_4$ inch thick) of the ganache if you're using it. Cover the cake again and refrigerate until slicing.

# Cheesecakes: To Floss or
# Not to Floss

Much has been made in the last several years over the discovery that one can cut cheesecake with dental floss. Frankly, I was never very good at flossing my teeth, so it comes as no surprise to me that I'm no more adept at flossing my cheesecakes. The problem is that most cheesecake (springform) pans have a lip on the edge; and the lip prevents me from drawing the floss clear down through the crust the way they say to. No matter, because the whole idea of flossing cheesecakes seems pretty silly anyway. And nobody ever says whether you're supposed to use plain or waxed floss.

I like a plain old sharp, thin-bladed chef's knife to cut cheesecake; works like a charm. Here's how to do it.

First, your cake must be good and cold, chilled for at least 8 hours, more if possible. Position your cake on a counter somewhere near your kitchen sink. Have a tea towel ready to dry your blade with.

First remove the sides of the pan if you haven't already, and score the top of your cake where you want to make your cuts. Now run the blade of the knife under hot running water for 5 seconds. Quickly wipe it dry and make the first cut, cutting down through the crust.

Rinse the knife blade under the hot running water, quickly wipe it dry, then make the second cut. Continue in this fashion until the cake is cut.

Because cheesecakes are so thick and creamy, it's often tricky getting the first piece out. It helps to get a wedge-shape spatula under the piece and reinsert the knife on one side of the cut. If you gently lift-pull on both, you'll eventually wiggle it out.

# Amaretto Cheesecake

When I was baking cheesecakes professionally, this one was the most popular with Italian restaurants. The filling is unabashedly rich and creamy smooth, slightly off white because of the Amaretto. The almond crust underscores the theme of the cake nicely, but a plain graham cracker crust will do. Use only a good brand of Amaretto, like Di Saronno; some of the cheaper brands have a harsh edge that you can notice even through the rich custard. When peaches are in season, serve a few slices with each helping.

1 recipe Cinnamon Graham Cracker Crust with almond variation (page 132)

## FILLING

1 pound Philadelphia cream cheese, softened to room temperature
$^2/_3$ cup sugar
2 large eggs, at room temperature
1 large egg yolk
$^1/_2$ cup sour cream, at room temperature
3 tablespoons Amaretto
1 tablespoon cornstarch
$1^1/_2$ teaspoons pure almond extract
$^1/_2$ teaspoon vanilla extract

## TOPPING

1 cup sour cream
2 tablespoons sugar

Prepare the crust as described, patting it into the bottom and most of the way up the sides of an 8-inch springform pan. Prebake as directed, then cool on a rack. Preheat the oven to 325°.

In a bowl, beat the cream cheese and sugar until smooth. Beat in the eggs and yolk, one at a time, then blend in the sour cream.

Pour the Amaretto into a custard or tea cup and add the cornstarch. Mix with your finger to smooth it and get out the lumps, then immediately pour it into the filling. Add the almond extract and vanilla and blend gently but thoroughly.

Pour the filling into the cooled crust then bake for 60 to 70 minutes. When done, the sides of the cake should have lifted slightly, and the center should be a little wobbly but not wet. Transfer to a rack to cool.

Once the cake has cooled for an hour, combine the sour cream and sugar for the topping in a small, nonreactive saucepan. Stir, over very low heat, just until it is slightly warm and loose, about 2 minutes. Slowly and carefully pour the topping over the center of the cake, letting it run toward the edges. Jiggle the cake slightly, if necessary, to encourage the topping to move right up to the crust. It may not be necessary to use all of the topping to get good coverage.

Cool the cake thoroughly, then cover with foil and refrigerate for at least 12 hours before slicing and serving.

# Buttermilk Chocolate Cake with Mocha Chocolate Glaze

*Makes 16 to 20 servings*

Here's a favorite "plain" chocolate cake, "plain" as in good enough to stand on its own without gobs of frosting or any other enhancements—save for a drizzle of icing. Baked in a bundt pan, this is the sort of generous, welcoming cake the neighborhood ladies used to, and perhaps still do, bring to their weekly sewing circle or coffee klatch. The glaze is thin when it first goes on, but hardens into a glossy exterior as it cools. Serve with fresh coffee, regular and decaf.

8 ounces semisweet chocolate, coarsely chopped
$1/2$ pound (2 sticks) unsalted butter, at room temperature
$1^1/2$ cups sugar
5 large eggs, at room temperature
2 teaspoons vanilla extract
$2^1/2$ cups sifted unbleached all-purpose flour
2 teaspoons ground cinnamon

2 teaspoons baking powder
$^1/_2$ teaspoon baking soda
$^1/_2$ teaspoon salt
1 cup buttermilk

MOCHA CHOCOLATE GLAZE

$^1/_3$ cup strong black coffee
4 ounces semisweet chocolate, coarsely chopped

Preheat the oven to 325°. Butter and flour a large, 12-cup (10-inch) bundt pan, preferably nonstick. Set aside.

Put the chocolate in the top of a double boiler and melt it over, not in, very hot water. Whisk to smooth then set aside. Meanwhile cream the butter in a large bowl using an electric mixer. Add the sugar gradually, beating on high speed. Add the eggs one at a time, beating well after each addition. With the mixer on low speed beat in the vanilla and melted chocolate.

Sift the flour a second time with the cinnamon, baking powder, baking soda, and salt. With the mixer on low, alternately add the buttermilk and dry ingredients to the creamed mixture, beginning and ending with the dry ingredients.

When the batter is blended, turn it into the prepared pan and even the top with a spoon. Bake in the center of the oven for about 60 minutes, or until a tester comes out clean. Cool the cake in the pan, on a rack, for 10 minutes, then invert the cake onto a large cake platter.

When the cake has cooled make the glaze: Melt the chocolate with the coffee over very hot water in the top of a double boiler. Whisk to smooth, then wait several minutes so the glaze thickens slightly. Spoon the glaze over the cake, covering as much of the surface as possible. Slice and serve.

Store the cake covered, in a cool spot; a foil tent will do if you haven't a dome lid.

# Brownie Pudding Cake

*Makes 6 servings*

Soft, warm, chocolatey—that brief description of this cake is poetry to the ears (and mouths) of dessert lovers. Imagine a billowy layer of dark chocolate cake atop a smooth chocolate pudding; that's it! Serve with cold glasses of milk, or pass a small pitcher to pour over the top. Kids love to make this one.

$^1/_2$ cup (1 stick) unsalted butter
4 ounces semisweet chocolate, coarsely chopped
$^1/_2$ cup sugar
2 large eggs
1 teaspoon vanilla extract
$^1/_2$ cup unbleached all-purpose flour
$^1/_2$ teaspoon baking powder
$^1/_4$ teaspoon salt
$1^1/_3$ cups near-boiling water

Preheat the oven to 375° and bring a kettle of water to a boil. Get out an 8- or 9-inch round ceramic or glass casserole.

Melt the butter in a medium saucepan over low heat. Remove from the heat and add the chocolate. Wait about 5 minutes for the chocolate to melt, then smooth the butter and chocolate with a whisk. Whisk in the sugar, then the eggs and vanilla, until the batter is smooth.

Mix the dry ingredients in a small bowl. Stir them into the chocolate mixture until smooth. Scrape the batter into the casserole. Gently and slowly pour the near-boiling water over the batter. Bake for approximately 35 minutes. When done, the top cake layer will be cooked through, and the bottom layer will look like pudding.

Cool the cake on a rack for 10 to 20 minutes before serving.

# Jim's Flourless Chocolate Cake

*Makes 10 to 12 servings*

*Flourless,* for chocoholics, has become the buzzword to look for in chocolate cake recipes. It implies the correct minimalist thinking that fuels chocolate passions: The less there is to impede the richness and flavor of the chocolate, the better. Here's a cake that embodies the true spirit of that thinking. Jim is my friend Jim Dodge, the former pastry chef from the Stanford Court hotel in San Francisco, not to mention the author of two fine baking books. He says this was a real favorite of guests at the hotel during his tenure there, and I can see why: It's dense and smooth, almost silken in texture, and it delivers an intense chocolate experience with every bite. And it's a real cinch to make. What more could you ask for? The tough part is giving this sufficient time to cool and then chill before serving. Serve with Raspberry Sauce or Crème Anglaise (page 200 or 199).

6 ounces (1¹/₂ sticks) unsalted butter, at room temperature
8 ounces bittersweet chocolate, coarsely chopped
1 cup sugar
¹/₂ cup unsweetened cocoa powder
4 large eggs, at room temperature

Preheat the oven to 325°. Butter an 8-inch springform pan. Line the bottom with parchment or buttered wax paper. Cover the (outside) bottom and sides of the pan with a double layer of aluminum foil, to make it waterproof; if you have it, use wide foil. Pour about ³/₄ inch of hot water into a shallow casserole large enough to hold the springform pan. Place it in the oven.

In a heavy medium-size saucepan, melt the butter over the lowest possible heat. Add the chocolate and swirl the pan so the butter runs over it. Turn the heat off but leave the pan on the burner until the chocolate is melted. Remove from the heat and whisk until smooth. Scrape the melted chocolate into the bowl of an electric mixer. Mix the sugar and cocoa powder in a bowl then blend them into the melted chocolate on the lowest possible speed.

In a separate bowl, whisk the eggs just to liquefy them, then gradually blend them into the batter on the lowest speed.

When the batter is smooth, scrape it into the prepared pan. Place it in the center of the casserole and bake for about 50 minutes; when done, the sides of the cake will have risen somewhat, and the center to a lesser degree. The center may still look slightly undercooked, but that's okay.

Cool the cake in the pan, on a rack, to room temperature. Cover with foil and refrigerate overnight. When almost ready to serve, remove the sides of the pan and invert the cake onto a plate. Cut thin slices while the cake is cold, but leave the slices at room temperature for 10 minutes before serving with your choice of sauce.

# Chocolate Hazelnut Torte

*Makes 8 to 10 servings*

Rich, dense, and unabashedly decadent, this is a chocoholic's dream. You wouldn't make this more than a few times a year—or would you?—when you want something really special for dessert. This is made in a single layer, and iced with Chocolate Sour Cream Ganache. The light texture and sour bite of the ganache is a perfect match for the sweet, compact cake. Serve alone, or with a few fresh raspberries or sliced strawberries on the side.

1 cup toasted and skinned whole hazelnuts (page 20)
5 ounces semisweet chocolate, broken into big pieces
$^1/_2$ cup (1 stick) unsalted butter, softened to room temperature
$^1/_2$ cup plus 3 tablespoons sugar
4 large eggs, separated, at room temperature
2 tablespoons Frangelico or Amaretto
$^1/_4$ cup unsweetened cocoa powder
Chocolate Sour Cream Ganache (page 204)

Preheat the oven to 300° and butter an 8-inch springform pan. Line the bottom of the pan with parchment or wax paper and butter the paper. Dust the pan with flour, tapping out the excess.

When the nuts are thoroughly cooled put them in the bowl of a food processor with the chocolate. Process until the nuts and chocolate are finely chopped, but before the mixture starts to gather together, about 15 seconds. Set aside.

In a bowl, cream the butter using an electric mixer, gradually adding $^1/_2$ cup of the sugar. Add the egg yolks, one at a time, beating until light and fluffy after each addition, about 10 seconds. Beat in the liqueur. Stir the nut mixture into the creamed ingredients.

In another bowl, whip the egg whites until they hold medium-firm peaks. Add the remaining 3 tablespoons of sugar and beat for another 30 seconds. Fold the beaten whites into the creamed ingredients. When there are still some streaks remaining, sift the cocoa over the batter. Continue to fold the batter gently until it is evenly blended.

Scrape the batter into the pan and smooth the top. Bake on the middle shelf for 65 to 70 minutes, until a tester inserted in the center of the cake comes out clean. Cool the cake in the pan, on a rack, for 15 minutes, then remove the sides. Cool thoroughly, then cover loosely with foil and refrigerate until you're ready to ice the cake.

Ice the cake with the ganache. Cover with a large cake pan or something else that won't touch the icing, and refrigerate until slicing. If possible, let the slices sit on the plates for 15 minutes at room temperature before serving.

# Spiced Buttermilk Pound Cake

Lightly sugared summer berries on this soft, fragrant loaf cake makes a perfectly simple summer dessert or weekend breakfast. If you'd rather, instead of making one big cake, divide the batter between two smaller loaf pans and freeze one of the cakes for the following week. Check the smaller cakes for doneness after 50 minutes.

$^1/_2$ cup (1 stick) unsalted butter, softened
$1^1/_4$ cups sugar
3 large eggs
$1^1/_2$ teaspoons orange extract, *or* 1 teaspoon vanilla extract
   plus finely grated zest of 1 orange
2 cups unbleached all-purpose flour
2 tablespoons cornstarch
1 teaspoon baking soda
$^1/_2$ teaspoon salt
$1^1/_2$ teaspoons ground cardamom
$^1/_2$ teaspoon ground cinnamon
1 cup (scant) buttermilk

Preheat the oven to 350°. Lightly butter a 5- by 9-inch loaf pan. Line the pan with wax paper and butter the paper.

In a bowl, cream the butter, gradually adding the sugar. Add the eggs, one at a time, beating until smooth and fluffy after each addition. Mix in the orange extract or vanilla and zest.

In a separate bowl, sift the flour, cornstarch, baking soda, salt, and spices. Mix about one-third of the dry ingredients into the creamed mixture. Blend half of the buttermilk into the batter, followed by another third dry, the rest of the buttermilk, then the rest of the dry. Mix the batter until uniformly blended.

Scrape the batter into the loaf pan and level the top. Bake for about 65 to 70 minutes, until a tester inserted in the middle of the cake comes out clean.

Cool the cake in the pan, on a rack, for 15 minutes. Invert the cake onto a plate, then turn it back over so it rests on the rack on the wax paper bottom. Peel down the sides of the paper. When the cake is cool, finish peeling off the paper. Slice and serve.

# Lemon Cake with Wheat Germ

*Makes 10 servings*

The texture of this simple lemon butter cake is moistened—and the lemon emphasized—with a honey-lemon syrup spooned on the cake after it has cooled. The syrup eliminates any need for an icing, but for a decorative touch you can lay thin curls of lemon zest over the top of the cake. The wheat germ (which I bake with often; see box, page 45) gives the cake a little nutritional boost and slight nubby texture I like.

$^1/_2$ cup (1 stick) unsalted butter, at room temperature
$^2/_3$ cup sugar
2 large eggs, plus 1 egg yolk, at room temperature
2 teaspoons lemon extract
finely grated zest of 1 lemon
$1^1/_4$ cups unbleached all-purpose flour
1 teaspoon baking soda
$^1/_4$ teaspoon salt
$^1/_3$ cup toasted, unsweetened wheat germ
$^1/_2$ cup regular or nonfat plain yogurt

## HONEY-LEMON SYRUP

$^1/_4$ cup fresh lemon juice
3 tablespoons mild honey, such as clover or orange blossom

Preheat the oven to 350°. Butter and flour a 9-inch round cake pan. Line the bottom with a piece of wax paper and butter it as well.

Using an electric mixer, in a bowl cream the butter, gradually adding the sugar. Beat in the eggs and yolk, one at a time, beating well after each addition. Blend in the lemon extract and zest.

In another bowl, sift the flour with the baking soda and salt. Stir in the wheat germ. With the mixer on low speed, blend half of the dry mixture into the creamed ingredients, just until smooth. Blend in the yogurt, followed by the remaining dry ingredients.

Turn the batter into the prepared pan and smooth it out. Bake in the center of the oven for approximately 30 minutes, or until a tester emerges clean from the center of the cake. Cool the cake in the pan on a rack for 5 minutes, then run a knife around the edge of the cake. Invert the cake onto a serving platter and remove the wax paper. Cool to room temperature.

When the cake has cooled, make the glaze: In a small saucepan, gently heat the lemon juice and honey. Spoon the hot glaze over the entire surface; don't neglect the edge. Cover the cake snugly with plastic wrap and let it sit for at least 15 minutes before serving.

# Whole Wheat Pumpkin Pound Cake

*Makes about 10 servings (1 large loaf cake)*

This is one of those simple, reliable home-style cakes that could easily become an autumn standby around your house; it is around here. One of the things I like about this cake is how moist and rich it tastes because of the pumpkin, yet it really isn't all that rich. This is good a couple of different ways, either with raisins or chocolate chips; in case you've never tried it, pumpkin and chocolate are wonderful together. Serve plain, as a snacking cake, or with ice cream for a special dessert.

$^1/_2$ cup (1 stick) unsalted butter, softened
1 cup packed light brown sugar
2 large eggs, at room temperature, plus 1 egg yolk
$1^1/_2$ teaspoons vanilla extract
1 cup canned pumpkin
$^3/_4$ cup whole wheat pastry flour
$^3/_4$ cup unbleached all-purpose flour
1 teaspoon baking soda
$^1/_2$ teaspoon baking powder
$^1/_2$ teaspoon salt
1 teaspoon *each* ground cinnamon, ground cardamom,
   ground ginger, and ground nutmeg
$^1/_3$ cup milk
1 cup chopped walnuts, preferably toasted (page 20)
$^3/_4$ cup raisins or chocolate chips

Preheat the oven to 350°. Lightly butter a 5- by 9-inch loaf pan and line with wax paper. Butter the paper and set the pan aside.

# Germ Welfare

Young moms with little children often ask me how they can sneak a little extra nutrition into their cookies and other baking so their kids won't notice. I tell them about a little trick of mine: wheat germ. Wheat germ is the heart of the wheat, where many of the nutrients are, and so it gives a nutritional boost to everything you bake with it. Not only is it healthy, but it adds a pleasant chewy texture and nutty flavor to your baked goods as well.

Wheat germ can replace some of the flour in your cookies and other baked goods, often up to but generally not more than 25 percent of the total measure. For instance, in a chocolate chip cookie recipe that calls for 2 cups of flour, you can replace up to $1/2$ cup of the flour with $1/2$ cup of toasted wheat germ without making any other changes to the recipe. Using wheat germ will sometimes result in more browning than usual, so if you find that's the case lower the heat by 25 degrees.

This 25 percent replacement rule has worked well for me in cakes and quick breads too; see the Lemon Cake with Wheat Germ in the recipe on page 43.

Using an electric mixer, in a bowl, cream the butter, gradually adding the brown sugar. Beat in the eggs and yolk, one at a time, beating until smooth after each addition. Blend in the vanilla and pumpkin.

In a separate bowl, sift the flours, baking soda, baking powder, salt, and spices. Alternately add the dry ingredients to the creamed mixture with the milk, beginning and ending with the dry ingredients. Stir the batter just until smooth, then fold in the chopped walnuts and raisins or chocolate chips.

Scrape the batter into the prepared pan and bake the cake for 60 to 70 minutes, until a tester comes out clean from the center of the cake; there may, however, be a little melted chocolate on the tester.

Cool the cake in the pan for 15 minutes, then turn it out onto a rack. Peel down the sides of wax paper and let the cake cool to room temperature before slicing.

# Semolina Cake with Olive Oil

*Makes 10 servings*

I love this light, spongy, golden semolina cake, which is so delicately textured and ever-so-crunchy that any adornment more than a dusting of confectioners' sugar would be a distraction. It's the perfect plain cake with tea or coffee, but if you insist on gilding the lily, I can recommend orange sections tossed with a tablespoon of orange liqueur.

Don't worry that the cake will taste of olive oil; it doesn't at all.

**4 large eggs, at room temperature**
**$1/2$ cup sugar**
**finely grated zest of 1 lemon**
**$2/3$ cup semolina**
**$1/3$ cup unbleached all-purpose flour**
**$1/8$ teaspoon salt**
**$1/4$ cup olive oil**
**2 teaspoons lemon extract**
**$1/2$ teaspoon vanilla extract**

Preheat the oven to 350°. Butter a 9-inch cake or springform pan. Line the bottom with a circle of wax paper and butter it too.

Put the eggs in a bowl of hot water for 1 minute to warm, then break them into the bowl of your electric mixer. Begin beating the eggs on medium-high speed, gradually adding the sugar with the mixer going. Beat the eggs and sugar for 4 to 5 minutes (with a freestanding mixer; it will take longer with a handheld one), until the mixture is thick enough to fall from the beaters in a thick ribbon. Blend in the lemon zest.

In a bowl, sift the semolina, flour, and salt. Sprinkle the dry mixture over the batter about one-third at a time, gently folding it in with a large rubber spatula after each addition. Measure the olive oil and extracts into a cup, then quickly but gently fold the liquid into the batter. When the batter is uniform and free of dry streaks, scrape it into the prepared pan and bake for 30 to 35 minutes, until a tester inserted in the center of the cake comes out clean.

Cool the cake in the pan on a rack for 5 minutes, then run a knife around the edge of the pan to loosen the cake. Invert it onto a wire rack, peel off the wax paper, and cool completely. The texture is improved by overwrapping the cake snugly with plastic wrap and letting it sit at room temperature for at least a few hours, preferably overnight.

This cake will keep for 3 to 4 days at room temperature in a coolish spot.

# Dark Chocolate Fruitcake

*Makes 3 small or 1 large fruitcake*

Next to C rations, I don't think any food has been as publicly cudgeled as fruitcake has. While I never had good C rations—and I ate my share during 4 years in the navy— I've eaten some excellent homemade fruitcakes. Especially this one. I've always considered it a bit of a cheat to put chocolate in a fruitcake, but if that's the only enticement for some folks to try it, then why not? Here I soak an assortment of dried fruits and nuts in honey and rum overnight, then bind them with a dark chocolate pound cake batter. (I slip in a few chocolate chips too.) The batter is spiked with Kahlúa and coffee, which gives the cake a deep, mysterious flavor. You must let the cake sit overnight before you slice it, and it is actually better if you wrap the cake in muslin and soak it with rum for several days—or much longer; this will keep. As a holiday treat, with good coffee, this will make you a believer.

## THE FRUIT MIXTURE

**3 cups mixed dried fruit (choose your favorites, including currants, raisins, dried cranberries or cherries, figs, etc.), pitted if necessary**

1 cup coarsely chopped walnuts, preferably toasted (page 20)
$^1/_2$ cup rum
$^1/_3$ cup honey
finely grated zest of 1 orange or lemon

## THE CHOCOLATE POUND CAKE

$1^2/_3$ cups unbleached all-purpose flour
$1^1/_2$ teaspoons baking powder
$^1/_2$ teaspoon ground cinnamon
$^1/_8$ teaspoon salt
$^1/_2$ cup (1 stick) unsalted butter, softened to room temperature
$1^1/_4$ cups packed light brown sugar
2 large eggs, at room temperature
2 tablespoons Kahlúa or other coffee liqueur
1 teaspoon vanilla extract
$^1/_2$ cup unsweetened cocoa powder
$^1/_4$ cup strong brewed coffee
$^1/_4$ cup milk
$^3/_4$ cup chocolate chips
rum for soaking the cakes (optional)

One or two days ahead, put all the fruit and walnuts in a bowl, cutting any big or whole pieces into reasonable sizes. Douse with the rum and honey and add the grated zest. Stir, cover with plastic wrap, and set aside. When you think of it, give the mixture a stir.

When you're ready to bake the cake, preheat the oven to 325°. Butter three small loaf pans (the 3- by 6-inch size is perfect) or one 8-inch springform pan. Line with buttered wax paper, leaving an overhang of 2 or 3 inches.

Make the cake batter by sifting together in a bowl the flour, baking powder, cinnamon, and salt.

In a separate bowl, cream the butter, gradually adding the brown sugar. Beat in the eggs, one at a time, followed by the coffee liqueur and vanilla. Add the cocoa and mix it. Blend the coffee and milk in a cup and set aside.

Fold half of the dry ingredients into the creamed mixture, followed by all of the coffee milk. Stir in the rest of the dry mixture and mix just until evenly blended. Scrape the fruit into the batter—along with the chocolate chips—and fold everything together until the fruit is evenly distributed.

Turn the batter into the pan or pans, and smooth the top with a spoon. Bake for about 45 minutes for the smaller loaves, up to 2 hours for the large loaf. It's difficult to tell if the loaves are done by inserting a tester, because it comes out with melted chocolate chips on it. But the cake should be slightly puffed and cracked in the middle. It should feel slightly resistant to light finger pressure. If it feels squishy, give it at least 10 more minutes.

Cool the cakes in the pans for 1 hour, then either lift them out of the smaller pans, or remove the sides of the springform pan. Cool on a rack for several hours. Wrap in plastic and store overnight before serving. For longer storage, wrap the cakes in muslin and saturate with rum. Store in a tin, adding a bit more spirits over the first few days as the cloth dries out.

# Coffee-Glazed Gingerbread

*Makes 8 to 10 servings*

I love a cup of fresh hot coffee with gingerbread, which made me wonder how gingerbread would taste with a coffee glaze. So I tried it, and I liked it! The glaze saturates the top quarter-inch or so of the cake, leaving what seems to be a layer of coffee icing. The gingerbread itself has fresh minced ginger, so this cake is full of big, deep flavors. Try this with the Pumpkin Ice Cream (page 177) for a special treat; butter pecan, coffee, or vanilla ice cream are good with this too.

$^3/_4$ cup strong brewed coffee
$1^1/_2$ tablespoons fresh minced ginger
$^1/_4$ cup ($^1/_2$ stick) unsalted butter, cut into $^1/_4$-inch pieces
$^1/_2$ cup unsulphured molasses
$^1/_2$ cup packed light brown sugar
2 large eggs, lightly beaten
1 cup unbleached all-purpose flour
1 cup whole wheat pastry flour
1 teaspoon baking soda
1 teaspoon ground cinnamon
1 teaspoon ground ginger
$^1/_2$ teaspoon ground cloves
$^1/_4$ teaspoon salt

<sup></sup>¹/₄ cup strong brewed coffee
¹/₄ cup coffee liqueur

In a small saucepan, heat the coffee just until hot to the touch then stir in the fresh ginger and butter. Pour the mixture into a large mixing bowl and let the butter melt. While you're waiting, butter a 9-inch round cake pan. Line the bottom with wax paper and butter it too. Flour the pan, tapping out the excess. Preheat the oven to 350°.

Stir the molasses and brown sugar into the coffee mixture. Stir in the eggs and set aside.

Sift the remaining dry ingredients into a large bowl. Make a well in the center, then add the liquid all at once. Stir until you have a smooth batter.

Scrape the batter into the prepared pan and bake the cake for 30 minutes, until the center is springy to the touch and a tester emerges clean from the center of the cake.

Cool the cake in the pan, on a rack, for 15 minutes. Invert it onto a plate, then immediately invert it onto a second serving plate so the top is up. Cool the cake for 10 minutes.

Warm the coffee for the glaze in a small saucepan. Pour it into a cup and stir in the coffee liqueur. Poke a dozen or so holes in the cake with a cake tester. Spoon, or preferably brush the glaze over the surface and sides of the cake; apply about one-third of it then wait for 5 minutes; do this until the glaze is used up.

Serve the cake warm or at room temperature.

# Steamed Black Chocolate Cake

*Makes 8 servings*

Steaming cakes is more than just a quaint idea from a bygone era; it changes the texture dramatically, in this case to a sort of moist brick close to a pudding. There's simply no way you can duplicate this in the oven. The cake is *black,* thanks to the molasses, coffee, and cocoa, all of which contribute to its deep flavor. Typically, the cake rises and presses against the foil, then settles and sinks somewhat near the end of the steaming; the structure of the cake has a hard time supporting the excess moisture. But don't worry, the cake will still be cooked through. And inverting it reverses some of the sinkage. The cake is so rich and moist, it doesn't need a sauce, just good fresh coffee to go with it.

$^1/_2$ cup strong brewed coffee
$^1/_3$ cup molasses
$^1/_2$ cup (1 stick) unsalted butter
4 ounces semisweet chocolate, coarsely chopped
1 teaspoon vanilla extract
3 large eggs, lightly beaten
1 cup unbleached all-purpose flour
1 cup sugar
$^1/_3$ cup unsweetened cocoa powder
1 teaspoon baking soda
$^1/_2$ teaspoon salt
$^1/_2$ teaspoon ground cinnamon
$^3/_4$ cup finely chopped walnuts

Butter and flour a $4^1/_2$- by $8^1/_2$-inch loaf pan. Put about $1^1/_2$ inches of water in a covered pot large enough to hold the loaf pan. Place a small rack in the pot for the loaf pan to sit on. Bring the water to a boil then turn off the heat.

Heat the coffee, molasses, and butter in a heavy medium saucepan. When the butter has melted, remove from the heat and add the chocolate. Wait for 5 minutes, until the chocolate melts, then remove from the heat. Whisk to smooth, then cool for 15 minutes. After 15 minutes, whisk in the vanilla and eggs.

In a large bowl, sift together the dry ingredients then mix in the chopped nuts. Make a well in the dry mixture then add the liquid. Stir until evenly blended.

Wait for 5 minutes, stir briefly, then scrape the batter into the buttered pan. Cover very snugly with a piece of buttered foil, then enclose the entire pan with one long sheet of foil, crimping the seams to keep water out. Place the pan on the rack. Check the level of the water; it shouldn't come up any higher than halfway on the pan. Turn the heat on and bring to a simmer.

Steam the cake, covered tightly, for 2 hours over very low heat; the water should barely simmer, not boil. Keep the lid on the pot; don't be tempted to fuss over or check it, though you should check the water level once after an hour, and add more if necessary. After 2 hours, pull back the foil and insert a tester in the center of the cake. It should come out clean.

Cool the cake in the pan for 10 minutes. Run a knife around the edge, then invert onto a plate. Cool to room temperature before slicing and serving. Keep leftovers covered, in the fridge—this cake is a good keeper.

# French Sugar Cake

This is not a cake in the traditional sense, but more of a thin, yeasted biscuit; the French call it a *galette*. *Please* don't be put off by the addition of yeast: There's only 15 seconds of kneading involved. The dough can be mixed in the food processor, and made in half the time it takes to make even the simplest traditional cake. This is a plain cake, with a slightly dry texture; leftovers are especially good the next day. Warm, it's excellent with fresh berries in season and a dab of whipped cream. You can use a wedge of this cake for your favorite shortcakes, or serve it with a little ice cream or mascarpone cheese on the side.

## DOUGH

1 package (1 scant tablespoon) active dry yeast
$^1/_4$ cup lukewarm water
$2^1/_4$ cups unbleached all-purpose flour
2 tablespoons sugar
$^1/_2$ teaspoon salt
$^1/_4$ cup ($^1/_2$ stick) cold unsalted butter, cut into $^1/_4$-inch
  pieces
$^1/_3$ cup milk
1 large egg, lightly beaten
1 teaspoon vanilla extract

## TOPPING

2 tablespoons unsalted butter, softened
2 tablespoons sugar

In a small bowl, sprinkle the yeast over the water. Set aside.

In the bowl of a food processor, combine the flour, sugar, and salt. Pulse briefly to mix. Add the butter and pulse the machine several more times, until the mixture resembles a coarse meal. Add the milk, egg, and vanilla to the yeast. With the processor running, add the liquid in a stream until the dough pulls together in a damp mass, about 10 seconds.

Empty the contents onto a lightly floured counter and knead gently about 15 times. Shape the dough into a ball then flatten it into a disk about $^3/_4$ inch thick. Slip the dough into a plastic bag and refrigerate for 30 minutes.

On a lightly floured counter, roll the dough into a large circle or oval about $^1/_4$ inch thick. Transfer to a lightly buttered baking sheet. Turn 1 inch of the perimeter under, and flatten it with the tines of a fork to make a slightly raised, decorative edge. Set aside in a cool spot for 15 minutes.

Adjust your oven rack to the center position and preheat the oven to 425°.

For the topping, smear the butter over the entire surface, then sprinkle with the sugar. Poke the surface with a fork several times (to let off steam trapped below). Bake for 15 minutes, until the cake is golden brown all over. Check about midway through, to make sure it isn't puffing up in the center. If so, poke again with a fork.

Slide the cake onto a rack and cool briefly before slicing. Wrap leftovers in a plastic bag.

# Apricot Sugar Cake

*Makes up to 10 servings*

This is essentially an apricot upside-down cake, using the previous French Sugar Cake to cover the fruit. The apricots are peeled, then cooked for a few minutes in a skillet with brown sugar and butter. If you're a good flipper, you can invert the cake out of the pan onto a platter; this is easier said than done with such a big skillet, and you have to be careful not to drip hot juice down your arm. (Wear long sleeves and oven mitts.) On the other hand, you can simply serve it right side up. Up or down, serve with vanilla ice cream.

1 recipe French Sugar Cake dough made with an extra 2
  tablespoons sugar (page 52)
$2^1/_2$ pounds fresh ripe apricots
$^1/_4$ cup ($^1/_2$ stick) unsalted butter
$^1/_2$ cup packed light brown sugar
$^1/_4$ teaspoon ground nutmeg
milk to brush on the cake
2 tablespoons granulated sugar

Prepare the cake dough as directed, refrigerating for not less than 30 minutes.

While the dough chills, bring a saucepan of water to a boil. Lower a trial apricot into the gently boiling water for 15 seconds, then remove it with a slotted spoon. Wait for 1 minute, then score the skin with a paring knife and pull the skin off. If it doesn't peel off easily, increase the immersion time until you can peel it easily. Peel all the apricots, then cut them in half along their natural crevice. Remove the pits. Preheat the oven to 400°.

Melt the butter in a heavy 12-inch skillet. Stir in the brown sugar and bring the mixture to a boil; boil for 1 minute. Turn the heat to low, then lay the apricots in the skillet, rounded sides down; you should have plenty to keep the arrangement good and tight. Turn the heat back up and cook the apricots for 5 minutes; the liquid in the pan will turn into a bubbly syrup. Sprinkle the apricots with the nutmeg and remove from the heat.

On a lightly floured sheet of wax paper, roll the dough into a circle a little larger than the skillet. Invert the dough over the apricots and peel off the paper. Brush the surface of the dough with milk, then sprinkle the granulated sugar over the dough. Bake for 20 to 25 minutes, until the cake is golden brown and done.

Wait a minute or two, then invert the cake onto a platter; or simply slice and serve. Either way, the cake should cool for about 15 to 30 minutes before serving.

# *Butter Yeast Cake*

### *Makes 10 servings*

Eggs and yeast leaven this simple cake with a soft, golden crumb. In its most basic form, the cake is just cut into wedges and served with fresh sliced juicy fruit—peaches, plums, strawberries, or fruit compote. The wedges can be halved and spread with sweetened cream cheese or mascarpone, or preserves. In the fancier version that follows, the cake is spooned with a sweet rum syrup and spread with jam, then served with sweetened whipped cream. Don't be intimidated by the yeast; this is no more difficult to make than any other cake. If you have a large KitchenAid-type mixer, this is a breeze.

> $^3/_4$ cup lukewarm water
> one $^1/_4$-ounce package (1 scant tablespoon) active dry yeast
> 2 tablespoons sugar, plus extra for topping

2 large eggs, plus 2 egg yolks, at room temperature
1 teaspoon vanilla extract
3 cups unbleached all-purpose flour
$^1/_2$ cup (1 stick) unsalted butter, softened
$1^1/_4$ teaspoons salt

Pour the water into a mixing bowl and sprinkle the yeast over it. (If you have a standup mixer with a paddle attachment, use the bowl from it.) Wait a few minutes for the yeast to dissolve, then whisk in the sugar, eggs, yolks, and vanilla. Stir $2^1/_2$ cups of the flour into the liquid. If you're using an electric mixer, stir the dough on the lowest speed with the paddle attachment for 3 to 4 minutes. If you're mixing by hand, beat the dough vigorously with a wooden spoon for about 2 minutes. Cover the dough with plastic wrap and let it rise in a warm, draft-free spot for 1 hour.

While the dough rises, brush a 9-inch round cake pan that's 2 inches deep with melted butter. Dust with flour then freeze for 10 minutes. Brush with melted butter and flour again. Refrigerate.

After an hour, break the soft butter into several big globs and stir it into the dough along with the salt. Gradually add the remaining $^1/_2$ cup of flour, beating the dough by hand for another minute, or with the mixer—on low—for another 2 minutes. (If by hand, I find a large, heavy-duty rubber spatula excellent for this stage.)

Scrape the dough into the prepared pan and let it sit for 5 minutes. Flour your fingertips then gently pat the dough out evenly in the pan; it will fill the pan by about one-third. Cover with foil and let rise in a warm, draft-free spot until doubled in bulk, 1 to 2 hours. Preheat the oven to 375° near the end of its rise.

When the cake has doubled, sprinkle the top of it lightly with sugar and bake for 40 to 45 minutes, until the top is a rich golden brown.

Cool the cake in the pan, on a rack, for 5 minutes then carefully invert it onto a plate then back onto the rack so the top is up. Cool for at least 30 minutes before slicing into wedges.

# Pulling a Fast One

Do you know any cooks who can materialize a fantastic dessert on the spur of the moment? Who seem to have a full cookie jar, a freshly baked crisp, and a steaming pot of coffee on the table when you walk in the front door? These apparently superhuman cooks are no more gifted than you or I; they're just better prepared. They stock up on pantry items, and throw an extra batch of cookie dough in the freezer when they bake. You can develop this knack too by cultivating a preparedness mentality. Here are a few suggestions to get you started.

—*Say It with Fruit.* Good fruit is the simplest of desserts, and a sumptuous fruit bowl is an inviting sight for your guests. Good apples, pears, and bananas are available most of the year. Add refrigerated grapes and melons, and you have an enticing selection.

—*Better Yet, Say It with Fruit and Cheese.* Keep a selection of fruit-friendly cheeses on hand. The Cheddars are perfect with tart juicy apples and pears, and the blue-veined cheeses are just right with pears. Plums love a creamy Gorgonzola. And a buttery Gouda works with just about anything. Let your cheeses sit at room temperature for at least 30 minutes before serving for best flavor.

—*Freeze a Shell* . . . When you make a pie pastry, make up an extra or two and freeze them to use later (see page 131). Cuts your time to a hot fresh pie in half.

. . . *And a Topping Too.* Any crisp or pie crumb topping is easily doubled or tripled. Double bag the crumbs and keep them in the freezer. You don't even have to thaw them before using.

—*Bag a Mix.* When you make cookies, double the dry ingredients. Bag and freeze it—with the appropriate identification—and you'll save a step next time. Or just double the entire recipe and bag up half for later.

—*Stash a Sack of Nuts.* Bowls of nuts-in-the-shell have a timeless appeal. Get some sturdy nutcrackers and nutpicks to make the going easier. Serve with an assortment of dried fruits in wooden bowls.

—*Indulge a Chocoholic.* Well wrapped, a good piece of bittersweet chocolate will keep for a long time in a cool spot. When you need it, chop coarsely and serve alone or with a small plate of raisins, fresh strawberries, fresh or dried pears.

# What Else Can You Do with a Sponge Cake?

Let us count the ways. . . .

—You can smear it, of course, with your favorite icing or frosting. Use it as a single layer, or halve it and double your fun.

—Or slather it with lightly sweetened whipped cream and top it with fresh seasonal berries; strawberries are the best!

—You can surround it with fruit compote, or fresh sugared berries. Or dab some fruit preserves right on top.

—Trifles are fun, and easy. Arrange thin slices of sponge cake in the bottom of dessert bowls. Cover with Crème Anglaise (page 199) and fresh seasonal berries. To keep it even simpler, use plain (slightly sweetened) yogurt or fruit yogurt instead of the Crème Anglaise.

—You can do the chocolate thing and ice it with either the Chocolate or White Chocolate Sour Cream Ganache (see pages 204 and 205). Especially nice if you use two layers and spread raspberry jam in the center.

—Soak it with hot flavored syrup, like the Honey-Lemon Syrup on page 43. Or use your favorite liqueur.

—Or just take it *really* easy and dust the top with confectioners' sugar.

# Drunken Yeast Cake

This cake, a sort of savarin without the ring, is saturated with a rum and orange liqueur syrup. The top is then spread with preserves; I like orange marmalade or peach, though I can't really think of a preserve that wouldn't work just fine. If you like an even boozier, moister cake, brush extra rum over the surface before you spread the preserves on top. And if it doesn't seem like too much trouble, consider serving orange sections on the side of each portion. Make this a day ahead if you like; it will keep just fine.

**1 recipe Butter Yeast Cake (page 54)**

## SYRUP

**1 cup water**
**$^1/_2$ cup sugar**
**$^1/_3$ cup dark rum**
**$^1/_3$ cup Grand Marnier or other good orange liqueur**
**juice of $^1/_2$ lemon**
**one 10- or 12-ounce jar orange marmalade, peach**
  **preserves, or other preserves**
**sweetened whipped cream for garnish**

Prepare and bake the cake as directed. Once it has nearly cooled, slice off the domed upper section of the cake with a long serrated knife. This will leave you with what looks like a regular cake layer with a flat top. (Cut the top into wedges and use it as a snack).

Heat the water and sugar in a small saucepan, bringing the mixture to a simmer. Simmer for 3 minutes, stirring occasionally, then pour the liquid into a bowl. Stir in the rum, liqueur, and lemon juice.

Put the cake on a large cake plate, preferably one with a lip to catch any excess syrup that might run off. (The cake plate shouldn't be the exact size as the cake, because the cake will expand when it soaks up the syrup.) Ladle about half the syrup over the cake, covering the entire surface. Wait for 5 minutes, then spoon the rest of the syrup over the cake. Cover the cake with plastic wrap and refrigerate for at least 30 minutes.

About 15 minutes before serving, warm the preserves in a saucepan just to loosen them up, then spread them evenly over the surface of the cake. Slice and serve with lightly sweetened whipped cream.

# Genoise

*Makes about 8 servings*

A genoise, or basic sponge cake, is one of the fundamentals of dessert making. You see recipes that are more or less sweet, or contain varying amounts of butter (never too much, however), but the technique is basically always the same: Eggs and sugar are beaten to a great volume, then the flour and butter are folded in. This is so much simpler to make with a freestanding mixer, such as the KitchenAid, than it is with a hand-held mixer, with which it will take perhaps twice as long for the sugar and eggs to reach the proper volume. It might take you several tries to get this down perfectly, but don't despair. Just take care to fold the ingredients gently yet thoroughly. And be patient beating the eggs. Even with a freestanding mixer, they will take a good 4 to 6 minutes to quadruple in volume.

> 5 large eggs, at room temperature
> $^1/_2$ cup sugar
> pinch of salt
> 1 teaspoon vanilla extract
> 1 cup sifted unbleached all-purpose flour
> $^1/_4$ cup ($^1/_2$ stick) unsalted butter, melted and cooled to
>   lukewarm

Preheat the oven to 350°. Butter a 10-inch cake or springform pan. Line the bottom with a circle of wax paper and butter and flour it also.

Put the eggs in a bowl of very warm water for 1 minute to warm them slightly, then break them into your mixing bowl. Begin beating the eggs on medium-high speed, gradually adding the sugar and salt with the mixer going. Turn the mixer onto high speed and continue to beat for another 4 to 6 minutes, until the batter is quadrupled in volume and forms a thick ribbon when it falls from the beater. Add the vanilla and beat for a few more seconds.

Sift the flour directly over the beaten eggs about one-third at a time, gently folding it in with a large rubber spatula after each addition. When there are no more visible streaks of flour, gently fold in the melted butter about half at a time.

Scrape the batter into the prepared pan and bake for approximately 30 minutes. When done, a tester will come out clean from the center of the cake and the sides should shrink away slightly from the pan.

Cool the cake on a rack, in the pan, for 10 minutes, then run a knife around the sides of the pan. Place a piece of wax paper on a cooling rack. Quickly invert the cake onto your hand, pull off the wax paper, then flip the cake onto the paper with the bottom of the cake facing down. Cool completely, wrap the cake in plastic, and refrigerate until serving.

# Peach and Raspberry Kuchen

*Makes up to 12 servings*

Here we take the basic genoise and bake it over a layer of lightly sweetened peaches and raspberries to make yet another simple fruited summer cake. You can use other seasonal fruits as well—including nectarines, apricots, and blueberries in any combination—but the procedure remains the same. As the fruit heats in the preliminary baking, you have just the right amount of time to whip up the cake batter. The best way to eat this, if you can wait, is to let it cool down for an hour or so. In that time the cake compacts and absorbs some of the fruit juice. Then the cake can be cut into neat pieces and served fruit side up, preferably with whipped cream or vanilla ice cream on the side. Incidentally, a nice variation here is to use whole wheat pastry flour instead of the unbleached flour when you make the genoise. It gives you a somewhat more moist and soft cake layer.

> 5 to 6 large ripe peaches, peeled and sliced
> 1 pint raspberries
> $1/3$ cup sugar
> 1 tablespoon unbleached all-purpose flour
> 1 recipe Genoise (page 61)

Preheat the oven to 350°. Butter a 9- by 13-inch glass or enameled casserole.

Toss the peaches, raspberries, sugar, and flour in a bowl. Scrape the fruit into the casserole, arranging it in a single layer. Bake for 20 minutes.

As the fruit cooks, prepare the genoise. After 20 minutes, scrape the batter evenly over the fruit and bake for another 30 minutes, until the cake is golden brown.

Cool the cake in the pan, on a rack, for at least an hour then cut into neat squares and serve fruit side up.

# Golden Shortcake Biscuits

*Makes 6 biscuits*

I've made dozens, perhaps hundreds, of variations of shortcake biscuits over the years, but none quite equal to this one. What most biscuits lack, I've decided, is not good ingredients—nobody seems to mind splurging for shortcake—but *drama*. A good shortcake doesn't just sit there pale and dutifully cut into a puckish round; it captures your imagination with its rich golden cast and irregular shape. So, rule number 1: Form your biscuits by hand, the way I do here. Rule number 2: Follow this recipe to the letter. Don't be concerned that the dough feels slightly damp; it's supposed to. Make these as close to serving time as possible; they're only at their peak for several hours.

2 cups unbleached all-purpose flour
3 tablespoons sugar, plus extra for topping
2$^1$/$_2$ teaspoons baking powder
$^1$/$_2$ teaspoon salt
6 tablespoons cold unsalted butter, cut into $^1$/$_4$-inch pieces
$^1$/$_2$ cup milk
$^1$/$_4$ cup sour cream
1 large egg, plus 1 egg beaten with 1 tablespoon milk for
  egg wash
$^1$/$_2$ teaspoon vanilla extract

Preheat the oven to 425°. Lightly butter a large baking sheet.

Into a large bowl, sift the flour, 3 tablespoons sugar, baking powder, and salt. Add the butter and cut or rub it into the dry ingredients until the butter is the size of split peas.

In a separate bowl, whisk the milk, sour cream, 1 egg, and vanilla. Make a well in the dry ingredients and add the liquid all at once. Stir briskly, just until the dough gathers in a shaggy mass. Cover the dough with plastic wrap and let it rest for 5 minutes.

Spoon a scoop of dough slightly smaller than a tennis ball into your floured hands. Roll between your palms to make a smooth ball, then place the ball on the buttered sheet. Make 5 more biscuits and place them on the sheet, leaving several inches between them. Brush the surface of the balls with the egg wash, then sprinkle each one with sugar. Bake for 20 minutes, until golden brown. Transfer the biscuits to a rack to cool.

*Variations:* Whole Wheat Shortcakes—Substitute ¹/₂ cup whole wheat pastry flour for an equal amount of the unbleached flour.

To make Banana Shortcakes—Put 1 large, very ripe peeled banana in a blender with ¹/₂ cup milk and blend to a smooth puree. Measure out ³/₄ cup, and substitute for the milk and sour cream.

# *Warm Berry Shortcake à la Mode*

*Makes 6 servings*

Every good cook knows the value of contrasts on the plate; here's a dessert that offers plenty of them. There's a warm berry compote, soft cold ice cream, crunchy shortcake biscuit—a big heap of playful, exciting contrasts. I'll leave it up to you which berries to choose; you'll need a total of two pints, and you'll want to choose what's ripe and in season. The best ones for the warm berry mixture are blueberries and blackberries. Raspberries may be used or not, but strawberries should be reserved for the fresh berry garnish. Tuck a sprig of fresh mint around the edge of the shortcake if you have one on hand.

**1 recipe Golden Shortcake Biscuits (page 63)**

WARM BERRY MIXTURE

**2 pints (total) blueberries, blackberries, and/or raspberries
juice of 1 orange
2 tablespoons sugar
¹/₂ tablespoon cornstarch
1 pint (or slightly more) good-quality vanilla ice cream**

Prepare and bake the shortcake biscuits as directed. Set them aside to cool.

Put half of each berry—a total of 1 pint—into a medium-size nonreactive saucepan. Add the orange juice and bring to a boil. Lower the heat and simmer for 5 minutes, covered. Mix the sugar with the cornstarch and stir it into the warm berries. Bring the mixture to a boil then boil gently for about 1 minute, stirring. Remove from the heat and cool for 5 to 10 minutes in the pan. Stir in the remaining fresh berries.

---

To assemble, split the biscuits and put the bottoms in shallow dessert bowls. Ladle a scoop of the warm berries over the bottom of each biscuit, then put a scoop of vanilla ice cream on top. Cover with the tops of the biscuits and serve.

# *Apple and Cherry Crisp*

*Makes 6 servings*

I love crisps, and I think just about everyone else does too. Even if you keep a modestly stocked larder, you're bound to have the crisp basics on hand for those occasions when you want a simple dessert in a hurry. I don't often make apple crisp out of season, but here is one notable exception, when the best sweet cherries appear in the market in early summer. Then I'm partial to this blend of apples and cherries, flavored with a splash of port. I cover this with a buttery sweet topping, and into the oven it goes. Let it cool down for half an hour before serving.

## FILLING

3 large firm cooking apples, peeled, cored, and sliced
2 cups halved and pitted sweet cherries
$1/3$ cup granulated sugar
$1/4$ cup ruby port
juice of $1/2$ lemon
2 tablespoons unbleached all-purpose flour

## TOPPING

1 cup unbleached all-purpose flour
$1/3$ cup packed light brown sugar
$1/3$ cup granulated sugar
1 teaspoon ground cinnamon
pinch of salt
$1/2$ cup (1 stick) cold unsalted butter, cut into $1/4$-inch
  pieces

Preheat the oven to 375°. Butter a 10-inch deep-dish ceramic pie pan.

Combine all of the filling ingredients in a mixing bowl and toss to blend. Turn them into the prepared pie dish.

To make the topping, mix the dry ingredients in a bowl. Add the butter and cut or rub it into the dry ingredients until you have damp, clumpy crumbs. Spread the crumbs over the fruit. Bake the crisp for 45 minutes, or until hot and bubbly. Cool for about 20 to 30 minutes before serving.

# *Apricot and Sour Cherry Crisp*

*Makes 6 servings*

In my earlier cooking years, all I knew of cherries were the dark sweet Bing cherries. I had heard of sour cherries, but not until my friend Annie Valdmanis picked a box for me from a nearby orchard did I have a clue as to how sour and special they really are. Actually, sour cherries have been around for ages; sour cherry trees were one of the first fruits cultivated in the colonies. But the cherries eventually faded out of the marketplace for the usual reasons: They blemish easily, don't travel well, and don't last long once picked. If you scout around you might be able to find a local source; an extension agent in your state may be able to direct you to an orchard where they're grown. They're worth looking around for because you just can't beat them for cooking. Thin skinned, full of juice, and deliciously tart, they're wonderful in pies and crisps. Here I've mixed them with apricots for a colorful sweet-tart summer dessert you won't want to miss. Serve with vanilla ice cream.

## FILLING

2½ cups sliced ripe apricots; it isn't necessary to remove
   the skins
2 cups pitted sour cherries (see Note)
½ cup sugar
juice of ½ lemon
finely grated zest of 1 orange
1½ tablespoons unbleached all-purpose flour
topping from Apple and Cherry Crisp (page 65)

Preheat the oven to 375°. Butter a 10-inch round deep-dish pie pan or shallow casserole; it should be ceramic or glass, not metal.

Toss all of the filling ingredients together in a large mixing bowl and spread it in the buttered dish. Spread the topping over the fruit. Bake the crisp for approximately 45 to 50 minutes, until bubbly hot throughout. Transfer the dish to a rack and cool for at least 20 minutes before serving.

*Note:* To pit cherries, poke the point of a cake tester, or a paper clip, through the stem end and push the pit out.

# *Peach Blackberry Crisp*

*Makes 6 to 8 servings*

We're blessed with an abundance of wild blackberries in the mountains of New Hampshire, and they make an excellent crisp with good peaches, which unfortunately are a bit harder to come by. Given the supply conundrum, it would make more sense to flip the proportions around here—more blackberries than peaches—but I've tried it and the effect is somewhat overwhelming; a few blackberries enhance the peaches with a splash of color and occasional burst of flavor, but a dearth of peaches gets lost in an abundance of blackberries. This special crisp topping incorporates toasted wheat germ, which besides being good for you adds a nutty overtone to the topping. It's made up right in the food processor as the fruit starts to bake, so this is a fast and carefree summer dessert.

## FILLING

4 cups peeled and sliced ripe peaches
$1^1/_2$ cups blackberries
$^1/_3$ cup granulated sugar
juice of $^1/_2$ orange
1 tablespoon unbleached all-purpose flour

## TOPPING

1 cup unbleached all-purpose flour
$^1/_2$ cup toasted wheat germ
$^1/_2$ cup packed light brown sugar

¹/₄ teaspoon ground cinnamon
pinch of salt
7 tablespoons cold unsalted butter
lightly sweetened whipped cream or ice cream (see Note)

Preheat the oven to 375°. Get out a 10-inch deep-dish pie pan or oval gratin dish of roughly the same capacity. Butter the dish and set it aside.

Toss the filling ingredients together in a bowl. Turn the fruit filling into the buttered dish and bake for 10 minutes while you prepare the topping.

Put all of the dry topping ingredients into the bowl of a food processor and pulse several times to mix. Remove the lid and scatter the butter here and there over the dry mixture. Pulse the machine several times, then process until the topping starts to clump together. Dump the topping into a bowl and rub it gently to make uniform crumbs.

After the initial 10 minutes, spread the topping over the fruit. Bake for another 30 minutes, until the crisp is bubbling hot. Cool on a rack, then serve the crisp with whipped cream or ice cream.

*Note:* Deborah Madison, that wonderful cook and author of *The Savory Way* (Bantam, 1990), mentions in her book a nectarine and plum crisp she enjoys with sweetened whipped cream flavored with orange-flower water. I loved the idea, and discovered it works beautifully with this crisp as well.

# Plum Cobbler

*Makes 6 to 8 servings*

Plums soaked in kirsch make a delectable and juicy summer cobbler. For the cobbler topping I use my basic Golden Shortcake Biscuits; I just use a bit more liquid in the dough, so it's loose enough to scoop over the fruit. This technique gives the top the earthy appearance of golden peaks and valleys. (You could also make the dough as usual, roll it out, and lay it *over* the fruit; that's the flatlander look.) There's a perfect time to eat juicy cobblers like this, 20 to 30 minutes out of the oven. At that point the fruit is still seductively warm, and the juices have thickened a little and begun to saturate the biscuit topping from below.

2 pounds (about 7 large) ripe plums, sliced
3 tablespoons kirsch or Amaretto
¹/₃ cup plus 2 tablespoons sugar

juice and finely grated zest of 1 lemon
2 tablespoons unbleached all-purpose flour
1 recipe Golden Shortcake Biscuits (page 63), made with
    an additional 2 to 3 tablespoons milk

Mix the plums, liqueur, $^{1}/_{3}$ cup of the sugar, the lemon juice and zest in a large bowl. Set aside for 15 to 20 minutes.

Preheat the oven to 400°. Butter a 10-inch ceramic deep-dish pie pan or casserole.

After the plums have soaked, mix in the flour then pour the fruit and its juice into the buttered pan. Bake for 20 minutes.

Prepare the Golden Shortcake Biscuits as the fruit heats, using the additional milk. Do not shape the dough; just let it sit in the bowl.

After 20 minutes, take the fruit out of the oven and spoon the dough over it in big globs here and there; keep the globs reasonably uniform and evenly spaced, but don't lose any sleep over it either. Sprinkle the remaining 2 tablespoons of sugar over the topping and bake the cobbler for another 25 minutes or so, until golden brown. Cool on a rack for 20 to 30 minutes before serving.

*Variation:* This is also excellent with a handful of pitted cherries replacing one of the plums. Increase the sugar slightly if you're using sour cherries.

# Question: When Is a Biscuit a Dumpling?

Answer: As often as possible! Which is to say, if you're looking for an effortless way to expand your dessert repertoire, any sweet biscuit—like the shortcake in the preceding recipe—can double as a fruit dumpling. Think about it: A dumpling is nothing more than a poached biscuit. All you need is something wet to poach your dumplings in.

What should you use? Well, what I have in mind is fruit—berries, pitted cherries, sliced apples, pears, or peaches. Put about 4 cups of fruit into a large nonreactive Dutch oven or pot. Add 2 cups of water, about 1/3 to 1/2 cup of sugar—depending on the sweetness of the fruit—and the juice of half a lemon. Bring to a boil, then simmer partially covered for about 10 minutes.

Spoon golf ball-size pieces of dough over the fruit, leaving several inches between them; you should be able to cook 4 or 5 dumplings at a time. Cover and simmer for about 8 to 10 minutes without uncovering; when done, the dumplings will seem moist, but there won't be any uncooked batter in the center. Serve some of the fruit and sauce with each dumpling.

# Comfort in a Cup:
# Custards, Puddings, and
# Other Smooth Moves

Here's a chapter devoted to comfort foods—soft, smooth desserts we can count on like an old friend. Comfort desserts are the ones Mom used to make when you were feeling blue, or as a special surprise, or when your favorite cousins were coming for dinner. Eating comfort desserts always made you feel good, and loved, and even okay about your brother, who at almost all other times was the biggest creep in the world.

Comfort desserts are soft, and rely on the most basic of ingredients. Bread, eggs, sugar, milk, and cream are the essential building blocks of comfort desserts, and it never ceases to amaze me just how much variety you can glean from such a limited store of staples. There are creamy custards like crème brûlée, fruit fools, and grain-based desserts like Indian and couscous puddings. There are also Bavarians, mousses, and frugal puddings made with slices or chunks of bread. You'll find recipes for all of them in this section.

Some people don't think comfort foods like puddings make a suitable choice for serving guests, on the grounds that they aren't fancy enough. I beg to differ. I've been to enough fancy restaurants lately to know that diners are paying top dollar to indulge in a little dessert nostalgia. Even aside from the silly distinctions between what's in and not, I think serving simple family foods to guests immediately puts them at ease, and lets down everyone's guard. As Marion Cunningham puts it in *The Fannie Farmer Cookbook* (Bantam, 1994), "We'd all be better off today if we admitted that there really is no such thing as gourmet cooking—there is simply good cooking. It takes . . . sophistication to know when to serve something simply. . . ." Amen.

It bears mentioning here that one of the only finicky aspects of egg-based puddings—and where many cooks experience less-than-perfect results—is that they shouldn't be baked too fast, at too high heat. High heat causes eggs to toughen, coagulate, and lose their ability to hold liquid. Have you ever seen a custard that "broke" from too intense heat? It's curdled and weepy, and the taste and especially texture are therefore not what they should be. If in doubt about your oven's temperature, always bake egg-based puddings on the low side.

Many of the desserts in this chapter are served and/or baked in their own dish. Having your own portion that you don't have to share with anyone else is one of the selfish little pleasures of comfort desserts; for once, you don't *have* to be a good boy or girl and share. Of course, looks aren't everything, but an attractive set of custard cups to serve your puddings and custards in adds visual appeal to the occasion.

# Bread and Butter Berry Pudding

*Makes 6 servings*

Here's a summer pudding the kids can make, almost as simple to throw together as buttering a piece of bread. Your favorite berries can be used in almost any combination—blacks, blues, rasps—and you can even throw in a few peach slices if you like. While all that warms, you butter slices of French bread, then arrange them over the fruit and cover with cinnamon sugar. If you can find it, brioche is actually the better choice for the bread; but French bread works just fine if that's all you have.

> 1 pint blueberries
> $^1/_2$ pint raspberries
> $^1/_4$ cup sugar
> finely grated zest of 1 lemon
> juice of $^1/_2$ lemon

## BREAD LAYER

> 6 to 8 slices of French bread, sliced about 1 inch thick, or
>   an equivalent amount of sliced brioche
> 2 tablespoons unsalted butter, softened
> 3 tablespoons sugar
> 1 teaspoon ground cinnamon

Preheat the oven to 375°. Generously butter a 10-inch deep-dish casserole or pie pan.

In a large bowl, toss the berries, sugar, lemon zest, and lemon juice. Scrape the mixture into the buttered dish and bake for 20 minutes.

While the fruit bakes, generously butter 1 side of each piece of bread with the softened butter. Mix the sugar and cinnamon in a small bowl and set aside.

After 20 minutes, take the dish out of the oven and arrange the bread slices snugly over the fruit, buttered side up. Sprinkle evenly with the cinnamon sugar and bake for another 20 to 30 minutes, until the fruit is bubbly and the top is nicely browned. Cool briefly before serving.

# Pumpkin Bread Pudding with Warm Chocolate Sauce

*Makes 4 large or 8 small servings*

I am a great experimenter of things pumpkin: I love it in quick and yeasted breads, coffee cakes, puddings, and custards. This is a cross between a pudding and a custard—something like a bread pudding but surrounded by a silken, smooth pumpkin custard. There are a number of ways to fiddle with this basic idea. You can vary the bread. Sometimes I use a light, eggy bread like brioche or challah. If I have whole wheat around, that's fine, too; the result is a little more compact. When I'm serving chocolate sauce, I like to spike the custard with a tablespoon of bourbon or Amaretto. But if I'm using Cider Whiskey Sauce, I prefer maple liqueur. (I use a brand called Maple Mist, unfortunately only available in New Hampshire, Maine, and Vermont); you could substitute bourbon. To keep things even easier, just serve with a small scoop of vanilla or butter pecan ice cream.

$3^1/_2$ cups (4 to 5 slices) bread, cut into $^3/_4$-inch cubes
$^3/_4$ cup canned pumpkin
4 egg yolks
$1^1/_2$ cups light cream
$^1/_2$ cup plus 3 tablespoons light brown sugar
$^1/_2$ teaspoon *each* ground cinnamon, ground nutmeg, and
    ground ginger
1 tablespoon bourbon or liqueur (see headnote)
1 teaspoon vanilla extract
$^1/_8$ teaspoon salt
1 recipe 5-Minute Chocolate Sauce or Cider Whiskey
    Sauce (page 198 or 206—see headnote)

Cut the bread and transfer it to a bowl; set aside.

In the bowl of a food processor combine the remaining ingredients except for the 3 extra tablespoons of brown sugar. Pulse the machine just until blended, or whisk the ingredients by hand in a regular bowl.

Pour about half of the custard mixture over the bread and toss. Set aside for 15 minutes. Preheat the oven to 375°. Meanwhile, generously butter up to eight ½-cup ramekins, or four 1-cup ramekins (the latter will give you a pretty substantial dessert).

Divide the saturated bread cubes evenly among the baking dishes. Stir the remaining custard then spoon it evenly over the bread. Sprinkle a little of the remaining brown sugar over each. Put the ramekins in a large, shallow casserole then pour enough very hot water into the casserole to come about halfway up the sides of the dishes.

Bake for 20 minutes, then reduce the heat to 350° and bake for another 15 to 20 minutes for the smaller dishes, or 25 to 30 minutes for the larger ones. When done, they'll puff just slightly and the centers may seem a tad underdone; that's okay. They'll finish cooking as they sit.

Transfer the dishes to a rack and let them sit for 10 to 15 minutes before serving. Serve with the chocolate sauce or cider whiskey sauce.

# Ethereal Orange Bread Pudding

*Makes 6 servings*

I like bread puddings that aren't too heavy, especially after a meal of any consequence. Here is a classic, delicately flavored with orange and so light it's like digging your spoon into a cloud. You can eat this as is, but I like it with fresh sliced strawberries. Or better yet, surrounded by Raspberry Sauce (page 200) and fresh raspberries. Incidentally, you can regulate the richness of this dessert as you please; some might prefer all or part milk, some might substitute a cup or two of heavy cream for the light. Whatever your diet can handle. Plan to eat this right as it comes out of the oven.

> 1 long loaf of French bread
> 4½ cups light cream
> ⅔ cup plus 2 tablespoons sugar
> finely grated zest of 1 orange
> 1 teaspoon orange extract, *or* 2 tablespoons orange liqueur
> 1 teaspoon vanilla extract
> 4 large eggs, plus 4 egg yolks
> 1 teaspoon ground cinnamon

Cut the loaf of bread on the diagonal into 1-inch-thick slices and set aside. You'll need about 14 slices.

Preheat the oven to 350°. Butter a large, shallow casserole or gratin dish; I like my oval one for this. Get out a second casserole large enough to hold the first one.

Heat the cream until hot to the touch. Pour it into a large bowl and stir in the $^2/_3$ cup of sugar, to dissolve. Stir in the orange zest and extracts.

In another bowl, whisk the eggs and yolks until liquefied. Stir a ladleful of cream into the eggs, then stir that back into the cream. Add all of the bread slices to the cream and submerse them for 5 minutes.

Lay the slices of bread in an overlapping fashion in the buttered casserole. Ladle the remaining cream over the bread. Put the casserole inside the larger one and add enough very hot water to come about halfway up the sides. Mix the remaining 2 tablespoons of sugar with the cinnamon and sprinkle over the top of the bread.

Bake the pudding for 45 to 50 minutes. When done it will be slightly puffy, and no runny custard should be evident between the layers. Serve right away.

# Mary's Shaker Pudding

*Makes 6 servings*

I was at an art fair when an older woman I know came up and slipped me this recipe, sort of on the sly, as you would slip someone a love note; she told me I must try this. I was appreciative, but frankly doubtful at first. The recipe looked a little rough around the edges, and lacked a certain refinement. But I'm a big fan of Shaker cooking, which has a refined simplicity of its own, so I tried it. And I'm glad I did. I can perhaps best describe this as a baked maple dumpling, and the result something like a pudding cake, with the cake part on top and a wonderful warm maple sludge at the bottom. My friend's original recipe had no walnuts, which I think adds a natural touch with the maple. Further fiddling with this would have changed the original recipe too much, but I think you'll love it just as is. It's important to let this sit for 30 minutes before you dig in, so the liquid has time to partially reabsorb into the cake and turn sludgelike. Serve with vanilla ice cream or cold light cream.

1 cup unbleached all-purpose flour
$^1/_4$ cup packed light brown sugar
$1^1/_2$ teaspoons baking powder
$^1/_2$ teaspoon salt

$^1/_2$ cup coarsely chopped walnuts
$^3/_4$ cup pure maple syrup
$^1/_3$ cup water
$^1/_2$ cup milk
$^1/_4$ cup unsalted butter, melted
1 teaspoon vanilla extract

Preheat the oven to 350°. Butter a medium-size loaf pan.

In a medium-size bowl, mix the flour, brown sugar, baking powder, salt, and walnuts. Set aside.

Put the maple syrup and water in a small saucepan and bring to a boil. Once it reaches a full rolling boil, remove from the heat.

Make a well in the dry ingredients. Add the milk, melted butter, and vanilla and stir quickly to blend. Scrape the batter into the buttered loaf pan and pour the hot maple water over the top. (The batter may float to the surface; don't worry.)

Bake the pudding for 40 minutes—when done, the cake part will be baked through, though there will be liquid on the bottom—then cool it on a rack for 30 minutes before serving.

# Couscous, Raisin, and Walnut Pudding

*Makes 6 servings*

Couscous is even quicker to prepare than instant rice and it makes a wonderfully textured, ricelike pudding. It also has an amazing capacity to soak up liquid, and keep soaking it up, which naturally affects the finished texture of the pudding. If you like it more compact, use the lesser amount of milk; if you like moistness in your pudding, use the greater amount. You can fiddle with this basic formula as you please. Orange zest and orange or lemon extract give this a citrus zing, which goes well with chopped dried pears or dried cranberries instead of raisins. You can use chopped pecans or almonds, instead of walnuts. Or include half a grated apple, if you please.

1 cup instant couscous (see Note)
$^1/_2$ cup coarsely chopped walnuts, toasted or not
$^1/_2$ cup raisins
finely grated zest of 1 lemon
$^1/_2$ teaspoon ground cinnamon

$^1$/$_4$ teaspoon ground nutmeg

1$^3$/$_4$ to 2 cups milk

$^1$/$_3$ cup packed light brown sugar, honey, or maple syrup

1 teaspoon vanilla extract

3 large eggs

Prepare the couscous.

Preheat the oven to 350°. Butter 6 individual ovenproof bowls or large custard cups; you may also use a small (4- to 5-cup) ovenproof casserole or loaf pan.

Fluff the couscous with a fork to separate the grains, then stir in the walnuts, raisins, lemon zest, and spices.

In a small saucepan, heat the milk and sweetener until hot to the touch. Remove from the heat and stir in the vanilla. Whisk the eggs in a bowl just until frothy, then gradually whisk in the milk.

Divide the couscous mixture evenly between the dishes or spread it in the larger dish; if you're using individual dishes, leave some headroom for the liquid. Cover with the heated liquid, and place your dish(es) in a larger shallow casserole. Pour enough hot water into the casserole to come halfway up the sides of the dishes.

Bake the pudding for about 40 minutes, until the centers are still slightly moist. This is best served soon after it is baked. Serve with a little pitcher of milk, light cream, or heavy cream.

*Note:* To make the instant couscous, either follow the package directions, adding $^1$/$_4$ teaspoon salt, or bring 1$^1$/$_2$ cups of water to a boil in a small covered saucepan. Stir in the dry couscous and $^1$/$_4$ teaspoon salt, and heat for 15 more seconds. Cover, turn off the heat, and let sit for 5 minutes. That's it.

# Apple Raisin Kugel

*Makes 6 servings*

Joan Nathan, author of *Jewish Cooking in America* (Knopf, 1994), calls noodle kugels the quintessential American-Jewish dish. She explains that kugels, a type of pudding, were first brought to this country by Bavarian or Alsatian Jews, who called them *schalet*. There seems to be an infinite variety of kugel possibilities—Ms. Nathan's book has no fewer than six—generally sweet, many made with vegetables, some moistened with sour cream, some cottage cheese, others with cream cheese. Though Ms. Nathan claims they're usually served as a side dish and rarely as a dessert, I prefer them for dessert, perhaps because I didn't grow up with kugels. In this variation I toss buttered noodles with a blend of sweetened cottage cheese and eggs, then fold in grated apple and raisins; you could use another dried fruit instead of raisins if you like. This kugel bakes up sweet, moist, and dense, not unlike a good bread pudding.

$^1/_3$ cup packed light brown sugar
1 teaspoon ground cinnamon
$^1/_2$ pound wide egg noodles
3 tablespoons unsalted butter, cut into several pieces
$^1/_2$ teaspoon salt
1 pound cottage cheese
3 large eggs
$^1/_2$ cup granulated sugar
1 teaspoon vanilla extract
1 apple, peeled and grated
$^1/_2$ cup raisins
finely grated zest of 1 lemon
light cream or lightly sweetened sour cream

Preheat the oven to 350°. Generously butter a 10-inch round casserole. Mix the brown sugar and cinnamon, spreading it evenly in the pan. Tilt the pan to coat the sides then press the sugar into the bottom and sides of the pan. Set aside.

Cook the noodles in salted boiling water until tender. Drain, then transfer the hot noodles to a bowl and add the butter. Add the salt and toss several times. Set aside.

Combine the cottage cheese, eggs, granulated sugar, and vanilla in the bowl of a food processor and process for 20 to 30 seconds, until smooth. Fold the cottage cheese mixture into the noodles, along with the grated apple, raisins, and lemon zest. Turn the mixture into the prepared casserole and bake for 30 minutes. Reduce the heat to 325° and bake for another 30 minutes.

When done, the kugel should still seem somewhat liquidy in the center—from moisture put off by the apple—though less so around the edges. Don't worry; as the kugel cools, the moisture will be reabsorbed by the noodles. Cool the kugel on a rack for at least 20 to 30 minutes. Serve warm or at room temperature, with a bit of light cream or lightly sweetened sour cream.

# Maple Indian Pudding

*Makes 6 to 8 servings*

This recipe first appeared years ago in a small book I self-published called *The Maple Syrup Baking and Dessert Cookbook* (see Note). The original version contained both spices and dried fruit, but over the years I've come to apply the less-is-more maxim to Indian pudding. Now I've pared it back down to the basics, which is where the founding cooks of my adoptive New England intended it. Hearty, sweet, and filling, this is a fine winter dessert—and a wood-stove classic if you happen to have a wood-burning stove. Serve hot or warm, in a pool of milk or light cream.

> 5 cups milk (use up to half light cream, for a richer version)
> 3/4 cup yellow cornmeal, preferably stone-ground
> 1 cup maple syrup
> 1/2 teaspoon salt
> 2 tablespoons unsalted butter, cut into several pieces

Preheat the oven to 300°. Butter a 9- by 13-inch casserole.

Pour the milk into a large nonreactive saucepan. While the milk is still cool, gradually whisk in the cornmeal. Whisk for about 10 minutes over medium-high heat, until the mixture starts to thicken. Stir in the remaining ingredients and continue to whisk for another 5 minutes; by now it should have the consistency of thin hot cereal.

Pour the pudding into the prepared pan and bake for 2 hours. Transfer to a rack and cool briefly before serving.

Note: The original book is now called *The Maple Syrup Cookbook,* published by Garden Way.

# Custards Rich, Custards Lean

Have you ever wanted to make baked custard, only to change your mind because the recipe looked too rich?

If so, take heart because most custard recipes—at least the ones I've made—are quite flexible when it comes to proportions of milk and cream. Fact is, so long as you include the eggs, your custard will set just beautifully whether you use half-and-half, milk, light cream, or heavy cream.

Naturally, changing the balance of the cream and/or milk will change the texture of the custard; cream-based custards are thick and dense, while milk custards are much lighter. It will also alter the custard's personality; a crème brûlée is best kept rich if you plan to knock the socks off your dinner-party guests. But for a weekday family meal, using whole milk in place of the cream in the same recipe is perfectly acceptable.

Cream or milk, remember to bake your custards gently—in a water bath—for best results.

# A Torch Worth Bearing

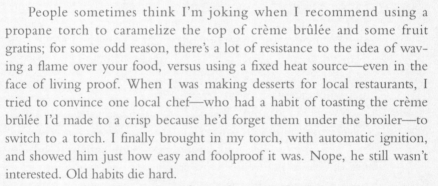

People sometimes think I'm joking when I recommend using a propane torch to caramelize the top of crème brûlée and some fruit gratins; for some odd reason, there's a lot of resistance to the idea of waving a flame over your food, versus using a fixed heat source—even in the face of living proof. When I was making desserts for local restaurants, I tried to convince one local chef—who had a habit of toasting the crème brûlée I'd made to a crisp because he'd forget them under the broiler—to switch to a torch. I finally brought in my torch, with automatic ignition, and showed him just how easy and foolproof it was. Nope, he still wasn't interested. Old habits die hard.

I say, anything that makes life simpler in the kitchen without robbing you of any intrinsic pleasure is fine. Caramelizing sugar isn't like kneading

bread, or chopping fragrant fresh herbs; I like to do those things by hand because they're sensual pleasures. Using a propane torch is no more or less gratifying than using your broiler; one is just simpler than the other.

So give the torch a try. You probably have one out in the garage anyway, and I know someone in your family has been looking for an excuse to buy an automatic ignition. That's an inexpensive little unit you screw into the propane tank to get around the hassle of lighting the torch with a match; all you do is turn the gas on low, pull a trigger, and you're in business.

When you caramelize something, put it on a baking sheet or another surface that won't be harmed by intense heat. Get set up before you actually turn on the torch, because you shouldn't leave a lit torch unattended, especially if you have kids around. Until you get used to the intensity of the flame, err on the side of caution, keeping the end of the flame back several inches from your target. Move in closer if necessary, and casually wave the flame over the surface like you've done this a million times before, rather than just blasting it in one area. You'll get the hang of it very quickly.

And you'll make crème brûlée a lot more often too.

# Ginger Custard

The one thing I look forward to as much as fresh summer blueberries straight off our bushes is ginger custard to go with them; I just plunk them on each new layer of this silken custard as I make my way, very slowly, to the bottom of the cup. Tastes great with fresh raspberries too. If I'm making this for the family, I don't bother to strain out the tiny pieces of candied ginger because I suspect they continue to heighten the flavor as the custard bakes. (My son Ben says: "The best thing about this custard is the pieces of ginger!") However, if you're serving this for guests who might question your breeding if you leave them in, just strain it through a sieve before you pour it into the cups.

> 10 pieces of candied ginger, each roughly the size of a
> bulky quarter
> $^1/_2$ cup sugar
> 2 cups milk
> 5 egg yolks
> $^1/_4$ teaspoon vanilla extract

Preheat the oven to 350°. Get out 4 custard cups and a shallow casserole large enough to hold them without crowding.

Put the candied ginger and sugar in a food processor and process for about 1 minute, until the ginger is cut into tiny pieces.

In a small saucepan, heat the milk and stir in the ginger-sugar mixture. Stir over medium heat, just until the sugar dissolves. Remove from the heat, cover, and let the mixture steep for 15 minutes.

In a medium bowl, whisk the egg yolks. Gradually stir the milk, then the vanilla extract into the yolks. (Strain at this point if you like.) Divide the custard evenly between the custard cups.

Put the cups into the shallow casserole, adding enough hot water to come halfway up the sides of the cups. Bake for 50 to 60 minutes, until the sides of the custards are set and the centers are still slightly wobbly. The centers should not be wet.

Transfer the cups to a rack and cool. Serve the custard warm if you like, or cool to room temperature. Cover and refrigerate until serving. Eat within 2 days.

# Orange and Toasted Coconut
# Crème Brûlée

*Makes 6 servings*

Here's a vanilla bean custard, flavored with orange too, and topped with caramelized brown sugar and toasted coconut. It may sound complex, but frankly it takes more care than actual effort to prepare. And of course, you could always pare this down to the essential custard, and forget about the topping. You can even skip the vanilla bean, and simply add a total of 1 teaspoon vanilla extract. As with all crème brûlée, you must make this the day before you plan to serve it, so the custard has ample time to chill. In summer, this is excellent with a bowl of fresh berries on the side; in cooler months, I'm more likely to serve it with an uncomplicated cookie. I swear by a propane torch to caramelize the tops (see Notes); it's so much simpler than using the alternative method, described below.

> 1 cup heavy cream
> 1³/₄ cups light cream
> ¹/₂ vanilla bean
> ¹/₂ cup granulated sugar
> grated zest of 1 orange
> 6 egg yolks
> ³/₄ teaspoon orange extract
> ¹/₄ teaspoon vanilla extract

## TOPPING

> 6 tablespoons packed light brown sugar
> 3 tablespoons toasted flaked, sweetened coconut (see Notes)

In a medium nonreactive saucepan, heat the creams until the surface shimmers. As it heats, cut the vanilla bean in half lengthwise and scrape the seeds into the cream. Drop the bean in too. Remove from the heat and steep for 15 minutes.

While that steeps, put the granulated sugar and orange zest in a food processor and process for 15 seconds. Transfer the sugar to a large bowl. Preheat the oven to 325°.

Whisk the egg yolks into the sugar. Remove the vanilla bean from the cream then gradually whisk the cream into the sugar mixture. Pour the liquid through a sieve into a pitcher or 4-cup measure, then stir in the extracts.

Divide the custard evenly between 6 custard cups. Place the cups in a large shallow casserole, leaving some space between them, and add enough very hot water to come about halfway up the sides of the cups.

Cover the custard cups loosely with tented foil, and bake for approximately 1 hour. When the custards are done, they may wobble slightly in the center, but they shouldn't be liquidy-loose. Transfer the custards to a rack and cool to room temperature. Cover the custards individually with plastic wrap and refrigerate overnight.

When you are ready to serve, preheat your broiler. Put the cups in a shallow casserole and surround them with ice and cold water, no higher than about two-thirds up. Evenly spread 1 tablespoon of brown sugar over the top of each custard. Run the custards under the broiler just long enough to caramelize the sugar; it will bubble and turn a deep caramel color. Crush some of the coconut in your fingers and sprinkle over each serving. Serve right away.

*Notes:* To toast coconut, spread it out in a thin layer on a baking sheet. Place in a 300° oven for 10 to 15 minutes, stirring occasionally, until lightly browned. Watch it like a hawk, because it can burn very easily.

Also, to caramelize the brown sugar with a propane torch, wave the end of the flame back and forth over the sugar for about 10 seconds, or just until the sugar bubbles and turns a deep caramel color.

# Creamy Lemon Tapioca Pudding

*Makes 6 servings*

Tapioca pudding is the first actual recipe I can remember making as a kid. I discovered it—and then began making it weekly for quite some time—at my neighbors' house, which might seem like a strange arrangement until you understand that Mrs. Kalish used to let me fold soft French vanilla ice cream into the pudding just before eating it. (My mother, poor sport that she was, wouldn't.) Today I've modified my method only slightly, lightening the finished tapioca with a little whipped cream; turns this all-but-forgotten American favorite into a smooth and creamy modern classic.

2¼ cups milk
3 egg yolks, lightly beaten

$^1/_3$ cup sugar
$^1/_4$ cup quick-cooking (instant) tapioca
finely grated zest of 1 lemon
pinch of salt
1 teaspoon lemon extract
$^1/_2$ teaspoon vanilla extract
$^1/_2$ cup cold heavy cream

In a large saucepan, combine the milk, egg yolks, sugar, tapioca, lemon zest, and salt. Stir continuously over very low heat for about 3 minutes. Increase the heat to medium and continue to stir and heat for another 5 or 6 minutes, until the mixture reaches a full boil; you will have to stop stirring for several seconds to see if it will boil.

When the mixture boils, remove it from the heat and set aside for 5 minutes. Stir in the extracts, then place a piece of plastic wrap directly over the pudding, touching it. Let the pudding cool to room temperature, stirring gently every 10 minutes or so.

When the pudding has cooled, in a bowl, whip the cream until it holds soft peaks, then fold the cream into the tapioca. Spoon the tapioca into individual dessert glasses or ramekins, and serve at once. Or cover and refrigerate the dishes until ready to serve.

# Maple Mousse with Toasted Hazelnuts

*Makes 4 to 6 servings*

This is light, creamy, and delicately flavored with the sweetness of pure maple syrup. In New Hampshire we'd consider this a special rite-of-spring dessert, to be served when the maple sap starts to run during spring thaw. But you can enjoy it any time of year. For a real treat, serve this with the Pecan Apple Butter Thumbprints (page 6).

4 egg yolks
$^1/_3$ cup sugar
1 cup cold heavy cream
$^1/_3$ cup cold pure maple syrup, plus a little extra for
   drizzling on top

$^{1}/_{2}$ cup toasted whole hazelnuts (almonds are fine too), cooled (page 20)
Frangelico (optional)

Put the egg yolks and sugar in a mixing bowl. Beat on high speed for about 4 to 6 minutes, until pale and fluffy. With the mixer going, gradually add the heavy cream in a thin stream; the mixture will thin, but then start to thicken again. When it is thick and mousselike, gradually add the $^{1}/_{3}$ cup maple syrup and beat until blended.

Divide the mixture evenly between custard cups, small ramekins, or serving glasses. Cover and freeze for 1 to 2 hours. (It can freeze longer, but if it gets hard, let it soften in the refrigerator for 15 to 20 minutes before serving.)

When ready to serve, finely chop the nuts and sprinkle them over the top. Drizzle with a small spoonful of maple syrup (and Frangelico, perhaps, if you have some on hand) and serve.

# Dairyless Orange Tofu Mousse

*Makes 4 servings*

I know several people who, for one reason or another, don't use dairy products or use them sparingly. If that describes someone you know, treat them to this smooth nondairy pudding. Not only does it taste great, it has a wonderfully creamy texture you'd never expect from tofu, the main ingredient here. Adding the little bit of the tahini makes it all the more velvety. I'm fond of maple syrup and orange together also, and if that sounds good to you, too, substitute maple syrup for up to half of the honey.

$^{1}/_{2}$ cup honey
$^{1}/_{4}$ cup water
$^{1}/_{4}$ cup orange juice concentrate
1 pound soft tofu
$^{1}/_{4}$ teaspoon orange or lemon extract
$^{1}/_{8}$ teaspoon vanilla extract
2 to 4 tablespoons tahini
ground nutmeg for garnish

In a small nonreactive saucepan, gently heat the honey, water, and orange juice concentrate, stirring occasionally until the honey dissolves. Remove the liquid from the heat, pour it into a glass measuring cup or something else with a spout, and cool to room temperature.

Lay the tofu on one of its narrow sides and cut it in half, so you have 2 thin slabs. Put them on a double layer of paper toweling and press on them with more paper toweling to blot up some of the water in them.

Pour the cooled liquid into a blender. Crumble the tofu and add it also. Blend to a smooth puree, adding the extracts with the blender running. Blend in 2 tablespoons of the tahini, then check the texture; it should be ultra-smooth and thickish. A little looseness is okay, because the mousse will firm up as it refrigerates. If it seems to need it, however, add another tablespoon or two of tahini.

Divide the mousse between small ramekins or custard cups. Refrigerate for at least 3 hours, or place in the freezer for an hour (don't leave it in the freezer any longer, however; transfer to the fridge after an hour if not serving it right away). Dust with nutmeg and serve.

# Creamy Sesame Mousse

*Makes 4 to 6 servings*

Sesame mousse might not sound out of this world, but this is really wonderful. The sesame here is tahini, a buttery paste made from ground sesame seeds. If you've ever had halvah, the sesame paste candy, you'll have some idea what to expect when you bite into this; the texture, though smooth, has a slight dryness to it, which becomes even more apparent if the mousse gets too hard in the freezer. Best thing to do is make this about 2 hours before you plan to serve it, then freeze; that's just long enough for it to get good and cold, without turning too hard. And if you do need to leave this in the freezer longer, fine. Just take it out of the freezer and leave at room temperature for 10 to 20 minutes before serving.

$^1/_3$ cup water
$^1/_2$ cup sugar
$^1/_2$ to $^2/_3$ cup tahini
2 teaspoons vanilla extract
$^3/_4$ cup heavy cream

Heat the water and sugar in a small saucepan, stirring occasionally, gradually bringing it to a simmer. Simmer for 2 to 3 minutes, then pour the syrup into a bowl. Cool to room temperature. Cover and refrigerate until cold. (To speed the process up, you can always put the first bowl in a second bowl of ice and water; stir occasionally, until cool.)

When the syrup is cold, add $1/2$ cup of the tahini to it and beat on high speed with an electric mixer. Beat for about 30 seconds. You want the tahini mixture to get slightly fluffy and thickish, like eggs beaten with sugar. If it seems thin, add a little more of the tahini. If it gets too thick, add a spoonful or so of water. Beat in the vanilla.

Whip the cream until it holds soft peaks, then fold about a third of it into the tahini. Fold in the remaining whipped cream.

Divide the mousse between 4 to 6 custard cups or ramekins. Cover individually with plastic wrap and freeze. Serve semi-frozen.

# Blueberry Lime Fool

*Makes 6 servings*

I know several rich fools, but here's one I actually like. We begin with a lime custard, then fold in whipped cream and fresh blueberries. No counting calories, because you won't make this more than once or twice a year anyway, though I know you'll be tempted to. If you make the lime custard a day ahead, you can assemble this in 5 minutes. Serve after a light summer meal, with shortbread cookies.

> 1 large egg, plus 4 large egg yolks
> $1/2$ cup fresh lime juice
> 1 cup sugar
> 4 tablespoons ($1/2$ stick) cold unsalted butter, cut into
>    $1/4$-inch pieces
> 1 cup heavy cream
> $1^1/2$ cups fresh blueberries

In the top of a double boiler placed over (not in) simmering water, whisk the egg and yolks. Whisk in the lime juice then the sugar. Continue to whisk the custard for about 10 minutes, virtually nonstop, until it thickens. Remove from the heat and whisk in the butter, one piece at a time, until smooth. Scrape the custard into a small bowl and press a piece of plastic wrap directly over it. Cool to room temperature, then cover and refrigerate for several hours, until cold.

To assemble, in a bowl beat the cream until it holds medium-soft peaks. Beat in half the custard until smooth. Whisk the remaining custard to smooth it, then fold it into the whipped cream with the blueberries, using only a few strokes; you want to see streaks of the custard in the final dish.

Spoon the fool into goblets and serve right away. Or freeze for up to $1^1/_2$ hours.

# Light Chocolate Raspberry Fool

*Makes 4 servings*

This is not particularly light from a caloric point of view, but neither is it overpoweringly chocolate, which would detract from the delicate raspberry flavor. All we do here is cloak the berries with chocolate whipped cream, flavored with vanilla and framboise or kirsch if that sounds good to you. You will need small, $^1/_2$-cup ramekins or dessert bowls to serve this from. However, if you like this idea and want to stretch it, use this to adorn pieces of the Buttermilk Chocolate Cake (page 37); you could serve up to 6 that way.

1 cup heavy cream
2 tablespoons sugar
2 ounces semisweet chocolate, coarsely chopped, plus extra
   $^1/_2$ ounce for garnish
$^1/_2$ teaspoon vanilla extract
1 to 2 teaspoons framboise or kirsch (optional)
$^1/_2$ pint ripe raspberries

In a small saucepan, bring the cream and sugar to a near boil, stirring, over medium heat. Put the 2 ounces of chocolate in a medium mixing bowl and pour the cream over the top. Wait 5 minutes, then whisk the mixture to smooth it out. Cool to room temperature, then cover and refrigerate for 1 hour.

After an hour, whip the chocolate cream with an electric mixer until it holds soft peaks. Add the vanilla and liqueur, if you like, and continue to beat until semi-firm; take care not to overbeat, however, or the chocolate cream will turn grainy.

Fold the berries into the cream, then spoon the fool into the dishes. Cover with plastic wrap and refrigerate for at least 1 hour.

When you serve the fool, take the extra piece of chocolate and grate little shavings over each portion.

# Biscotti Tiramisu

*Makes 4 servings*

This dessert is loosely based on the wildly famous Italian dessert, tiramisu. Instead of the traditional sponge cake, this one uses biscotti, either homemade or a good store-bought brand, if you can find one. The biscotti are broken into pieces, covered with a coffee liqueur mixture, then topped with a blend of mascarpone and whipped cream. A favorite variation on the basic idea is to drizzle Irish cream liqueur over the biscotti instead of the coffee and coffee liqueur. Don't sprinkle the liquid over the biscotti until just before serving; you want the biscotti to stay somewhat crunchy.

> 4 to 6 good-size biscotti, preferably almond flavored (page 13)
> $1/2$ cup heavy cream
> 3 tablespoons sugar
> $1/2$ cup mascarpone cheese
> $1/4$ teaspoon vanilla extract
> $1/2$ cup strong brewed coffee
> $1/4$ cup coffee liqueur

Break the biscotti into bite-size pieces and arrange the pieces snugly in the bottom of 4 shallow dessert bowls. Set aside.

In a chilled bowl, whip the cream, gradually adding the sugar as the cream starts to thicken. Continue to whip the cream until it forms soft peaks.

In a separate small bowl, stir the mascarpone to smooth it out. Fold in about a third of the whipped cream, then fold the lightened mascarpone back into the whipped cream. Stir in the vanilla extract.

Blend the coffee and coffee liqueur in a small bowl. When you are ready to serve, spoon 2 or 3 tablespoons of the coffee liquid over each bowlful of crumbled biscotti. Cover each with a generous layer of the cream and serve right away.

# Chocolate Pâte with Raspberry Sauce

*Makes 1 dozen servings*

Here's a decadent one for the holiday season, when you want to pull out all the stops. Though the presentation is stunning, the preparation is neither difficult nor time-consuming (the hard part is waiting 24 hours before it's firm enough to slice). What you end up with is a brick of velvety smooth, enriched chocolate that's almost too intense to eat alone; hence, the raspberry sauce, which provides a light, fruity contrast. You put a thin slice of the pâte down on each plate, and surround it with a pool of the sauce. You'll want to cut the pâte while it is good and cold, but leave the slices at room temperature for about 10 minutes before serving for best flavor.

> 1 cup heavy cream
> $^1/_3$ cup Grand Marnier or Cointreau
> 1 pound bittersweet chocolate, coarsely chopped
> $^1/_2$ cup confectioners' sugar
> 4 egg yolks, at room temperature
> $^1/_2$ cup ($^1/_4$ pound) unsalted butter, quite soft
> Raspberry Sauce (page 200)
> a few fresh raspberries for garnish (optional)

Line a $3^1/_2$- to 4-cup loaf pan with parchment paper or plastic wrap, allowing for a 2-inch overhang.

In a large saucepan, combine the heavy cream and Grand Marnier. Add the chocolate and place the pan over the lowest possible heat. Stir occasionally to melt the chocolate, about 10 minutes, then whisk in the sugar until the mixture is smooth. Remove the pan from heat and whisk in the egg yolks.

Transfer the mixture to the food processor and add the butter. Process for 5 seconds, scrape down the sides, and process for 2 or 3 more seconds, until uniformly smooth. Immediately pour the batter into the prepared pan. Jiggle the pan, to settle the contents. Cool to room temperature. Cover and refrigerate for 24 hours.

To serve, grasp the paper overhang and lift the pâte out of the pan. Unwrap, then slice the pâte with a warm sharp knife into pieces no more than $^1/_2$ inch thick. Slide the slice off the knife onto the plate and surround with sauce. If you have extra berries, scatter them here and there on each plate.

---

# By Fork or Hand:
# Crepes, Sweet Toasts, and
# Other Bread-Based Desserts

What the desserts in this chapter have in common is a supporting feature—some sort of wrapper, holder, or surface to contain an element that would be lacking on its own. But containment is only part of their mission. These supporting players provide bulk, contrast in texture, and bland balance in the presence of up-front flavors like chocolate.

Fresh store-bought crepes are available in the produce sections of many supermarkets now, and when you haven't the time to make your own you can count on them. On the other hand, if you haven't made your own crepes before, or in a while, you'll be surprised just how simple it can be. The ingredients are just buzzed all together in the blender, then cooked individually in a hot skillet. The technique is uncomplicated, and quite speedy once you've made a couple of trial crepes to get you started. You're never far from a quick dessert with crepes and a jar of good preserves on hand; jam-filled crepes dusted with confectioners' sugar are sensational.

If you have kids, I've included here a "crepe" made with store-bought tortilla shells; the kids will love it, and so will you. Of course tortillas don't have the soft, pancakelike texture of real crepes, but what they lack in sophistication, they make up for in sheer ease of handling. And once you gently heat them in sugar and butter, the differences seem minimal.

The popularity of toast-based savories like crostini and bruschette inspired me to apply the concept to dessert, I think with wonderful results. Toasts, I find, work beautifully with sweetened cheeses like mascarpone and ricotta, and both are terrific with the addition of fruit. In the same vein, I've put a sweet twist on focaccia with a grape version built upon a golden-brown homemade crust.

Finally, you'll also find here a couple of phyllo favorites, including an apple apricot strudel and baskets composed of layered phyllo leaves. They make pretty, graceful containers for fruit compotes, whipped cream and berries, and quickies like sautéed apple slices and Crème Anglaise (page 199).

# Basic Crepes

This is essentially the same crepe recipe I included in my previous book, *Country Breakfasts;* no use messing with a reliable recipe. Consider making these in quantity, and freezing them in batches, because with crepes on hand you're never far from a quick dessert. Once you get in the rhythm, these move along quickly.

A trick: Just before you flip the crepes, run your fingers under cold water or stick them in a bowl of ice water then quickly dry them off. Then loosen the crepe "tail" and flip with your cool fingers; works a lot better than a spatula, which tends to mangle them.

3 large eggs
$1^1/_2$ cups milk
1 cup unbleached all-purpose flour; for whole wheat
  crepes use $^1/_2$ cup *each* unbleached and whole wheat flour
1 tablespoon sugar
$^1/_4$ teaspoon salt
1 tablespoon unsalted butter, melted, plus a little extra for
  the pan

Put all of the ingredients except the butter in a blender and puree until smooth. Add the butter and puree briefly again. Pour the batter into a large measuring cup or pitcher and let sit at room temperature for 30 minutes, or overnight in the refrigerator, covered.

When you're ready to cook the crepes, heat an 8- or 9-inch nonstick skillet over medium heat. Rub a little butter in the pan with paper towels.

Ladle a scoop of batter into the pan, then immediately tilt and twirl the pan to spread the batter evenly around the bottom of the pan. Pour off the excess; from the time the batter hits the pan until the time you pour off the excess is no more than 3 to 5 seconds. Cook the crepe on the first side for 45 to 60 seconds, then loosen the "tail" (where you poured off the excess) with a knife; flip the crepe and cook on the other side for about 30 more seconds.

Slide or invert the crepe out of the pan onto a baking sheet lined with wax paper. Continue to cook the crepes in this manner, brushing the pan with butter between every other crepe. Place a piece of wax paper between each crepe. The crepes can be used right away, or you can let the stack cool then cover with plastic wrap and refrigerate for several days. They can also be frozen for several weeks—well wrapped in plastic—then thawed at room temperature.

*Variation:* Vanilla Crepes—Put the milk into a saucepan. Scrape the seeds from half a vanilla bean into the milk; add the pod to the milk too. Heat the milk to near the boiling point, then remove from the heat. Cover and cool to room temperature. Remove the pod, then proceed as directed.

# Crepes (Two Ways) with Frozen Peanut Butter Mousse

*Makes 4 servings*

Here you have your choice of crepes—raspberry jam or chocolate—served astride a scoop of frozen peanut butter mousse. Technically I'm not sure that this is a mousse since it doesn't contain eggs, but it's quite good, and light and creamy—perfect with the crepes—so why quibble about it? If you can't decide which crepe to serve, do both for each serving—one of the chocolate, one of the raspberry. Lay them on dessert plates, points touching, with a scoop of the mousse in the center. If there isn't time, you don't have to chill the mousse, in which case it will be more like a peanut butter whipped cream—also delightful.

## MOUSSE

$^2/_3$ cup chilled heavy cream
5 tablespoons sugar
$^1/_3$ cup smooth natural peanut butter
$^1/_2$ teaspoon vanilla extract

## CREPES

a little sugar for the pan
8 Basic Crepes (page 93)
4 to 8 ounces semisweet chocolate, grated, *and/or* $^1/_3$ to $^2/_3$
  cup raspberry preserves
2 tablespoons unsalted butter

To make the mousse, whip the cream in a small bowl, gradually adding the sugar. When the cream holds soft peaks beat in the peanut butter and vanilla extract just until smooth. Cover and place in the freezer for 1 hour.

To make chocolate crepes, heat a medium-size skillet over medium-low heat. Rub a little butter in the bottom of the pan, then sprinkle with several big pinches of sugar. Lay a crepe in the pan and cover the surface with grated chocolate. Wait for 10 seconds, then fold the crepe in half. Wait for 10 more seconds then fold in half again, leaving you with a quarter wedge. Transfer to a serving plate and make another. Serve 2 on a plate, with a scoop of the mousse.

To make raspberry crepes, spread 1 to $1^1/2$ tablespoons preserves over the surface of the crepes before you put them in the pan. Fold into quarters as for the chocolate crepe. Do up to 3 or 4 at a time, then melt about $^1/2$ tablespoon butter in a medium skillet. Sprinkle the skillet with sugar then brown the crepes for about 1 minute on each side.

# Crepes Mascarpone with Cinnamon Sugar

*Makes 4 servings*

This is the way I like to eat perfectly fresh summer fruit: alongside these soft, warm crepes with a big spoonful of cool mascarpone tucked inside them. The key to doing this right is sliding the crepes out of the pan and cooling them down ever so briefly before you tuck the mascarpone in them; the mascarpone has to be chilled ahead. Done correctly, the crepes are barely warm and supple and the mascarpone stays slightly cool. I love fresh sliced peaches or strawberries with these, to balance the smooth richness of the mascarpone. But any good summer fruit or berry will do nicely (or use the Chunky Summer Fruit Salsa on page 144). Since these don't really hold well, you'll have to serve them as you make them.

8 Basic Crepes (page 93)
1 tablespoon sugar
1 teaspoon ground cinnamon

MASCARPONE FILLING

1 cup cold mascarpone cheese
2 tablespoons sugar
$^1/4$ teaspoon vanilla extract
1 to 2 tablespoons unsalted butter
fresh fruit to serve alongside

Prepare the crepes ahead of time, preferably an hour or so. They're easier to work with if they've had a chance to sit.

Combine the sugar and cinnamon in a small bowl and set aside.

In another small bowl, briefly stir the mascarpone and sugar; don't beat it. Stir in the vanilla just until blended. Cover and refrigerate for at least an hour.

When you are ready to proceed, heat a medium-size skillet over medium-low heat. Rub a little of the butter in the bottom of the pan, then sprinkle the pan with a big pinch of the cinnamon sugar. Put one crepe in the pan and sprinkle lightly with cinnamon sugar. Let it heat for about 30 seconds then fold in half. Sprinkle again with cinnamon sugar then slide the crepe out onto a plate. Cool for about 15 seconds.

Put a heaping tablespoon of the cold mascarpone on one side of the crepe and fold the other half over it. Slide this quarter-wedge onto a serving plate and surround with fresh sliced fruit or berries. Continue for the rest of the crepes, serving 2 per person.

# Chocolate Soufflé Crepes

*Makes 4 servings*

A souffléed crepe is like a new romance: Once the steam wears off, you hope there's something very good there to sink your teeth into. My experience with souffléed crepes is that they can be every bit as capricious as love affairs. Chocolate seems to be the predominant exception, since it tastes just as good deflated as it does inflated; note the many recipes we see these days for "fallen" chocolate soufflé cakes. Here we fill crepes with a mixture of ground chocolate and nuts that have been mixed with beaten egg whites and cocoa. They're quickly baked in individual gratin dishes and served forth lightly dusted with confectioners' sugar. If they're in season, a small bowl of sliced fresh strawberries is a nice accompaniment.

4 Basic Crepes (page 93)

FILLING

4 ounces semisweet chocolate, coarsely chopped
$^1/_2$ cup walnut pieces
4 tablespoons granulated sugar
1 tablespoon unbleached all-purpose flour

$^1/_8$ teaspoon ground cinnamon
3 egg whites, at room temperature
1 (scant) tablespoon unsweetened cocoa powder
confectioners' sugar to sift on top

Prepare the crepes if you haven't already; they'll be a little easier to handle if you've prepared them ahead.

When you're ready to proceed, preheat the oven to 400°. Butter 4 individual oval gratin dishes or casseroles. These can also be baked on a baking sheet if necessary, then quickly transferred to dessert plates after baking.

Put the chocolate in the bowl of a food processor and chop for 5 seconds. Add the nuts, 2 tablespoons of the sugar, the flour, and cinnamon and process again until the mixture is finely chopped. Avoid overprocessing, or the nuts will become oily and the mixture will be clumpy.

In a medium-size bowl, beat the egg whites, gradually adding the remaining granulated sugar. When the whites hold medium-firm peaks, fold about a third of the chopped chocolate mixture into them. Gently fold the rest in, a third at a time. Sprinkle the cocoa over the mixture and continue to fold just until evenly blended.

Drape half of each crepe in the gratin dishes and spoon one-quarter of the mixture into each one. Fold the top of the crepe over the filling. Bake for 15 minutes, or until puffed.

Dust the hot crepes with confectioners' sugar and serve right away.

## *An Easy Chocolate "Crepe" for the Kids*

*Makes 2 servings*

This is an excellent recipe for kids, and anybody else who likes to have a little fun in the kitchen. And while it isn't something I'd be likely to serve guests, I'm almost embarrassed to say how much *this* big kid loves this superquick dessert. The "crepe" shell I use for this is a good-quality tortilla I buy at my local health food store. (I like the whole wheat ones better than the all-white ones, which tend to be gummy.) You simply heat the tortilla in a skillet with a little butter and sugar, which renders it amazingly soft and dessertlike; then melt chocolate chips over the surface and dot with raspberry jam. Fold and serve. That's all there is to it. Serve with lots of cold milk.

$^1/_2$ tablespoon unsalted butter
$^1/_2$ teaspoon sugar
1 thin flour tortilla
3 tablespoons chocolate chips
$1^1/_2$ tablespoons raspberry jam

Melt the butter in the middle of a large skillet over very low heat. Sprinkle the sugar into the pan, then place the tortilla in the pan. Immediately scatter the chocolate chips over half of the tortilla. Cover the pan for about 30 seconds (use a baking sheet if you haven't a lid) to melt the chips.

Uncover the pan and spoon the raspberry jam here and there over the chocolate. Fold the uncovered half of the tortilla over the other half, then lift the "crepe" out of the pan with a spatula. Cut in half and serve right away.

*Variations:* Kids are creative, and they'll come up with lots of variations to this basic theme. How about chocolate with chopped nuts, sliced bananas, or pears?

# Sourdough Pains au Chocolat

*Makes 2 servings*

I have long been a fan of Bernard Clayton's wonderful book, *The Breads of France* (Macmillan, 1985). In it, there's a recipe for chocolate-filled rolls—warm rolls with an oozing chunk of chocolate tucked inside—which have been a treat for French children for ages. I loved the idea so much I came up with this, a grilled version made with good sourdough bread. The sourness of the bread lends a subtle balance to the chocolate. These are meant to be eaten out-of-hand, with nothing more than a glass of cold milk. This can easily be multiplied to serve a number of people.

1 thick sourdough baguette
1 to 2 tablespoons unsalted butter, softened
2 ounces semisweet or bittersweet chocolate

Cut the loaf of bread on the diagonal as follows: Cut all the way through the loaf, then move the knife over half an inch and cut almost all the way through, stopping just at the crust. Again move the knife over half an inch and cut all the way through. You should have 2 slices of bread joined by a thin hinge. Repeat to make a second one.

Begin to heat a medium cast-iron skillet over a medium flame.

Butter the outside surfaces of both breads then tuck about an ounce of the chocolate inside each pocket. If the chocolate is on the thick side, you'll have to cut it in half so it fits tidily inside the pocket.

Grill the bread for about $1^1/_2$ minutes on each side, more or less, until golden brown. The trick is to brown it fast enough to get a nice golden crust before the chocolate starts to run out. Let the bread cool down for a minute or so, then serve.

# Crostini of Peaches, Cider Jelly, and Mascarpone

*Makes 4 servings*

Simple, elegant, *sensational*—this sweet, open-face sandwich has it all. Three seemingly disparate flavors are layered on crunchy toast, but in your mouth they blend in perfect harmony. Get the best loaf of country bread you can find; inferior bread doesn't do this justice. A sourdough is an excellent choice. Serve these with a glass of white wine.

> 4 medium-size slices of rustic bread
> 1 small jar cider jelly (available at health food or specialty
>   food stores, or the source on page 23)
> 8 ounces cold mascarpone cheese
> 4 medium-size ripe peaches, peeled and thickly sliced
> ground nutmeg for garnish

Preheat the oven to 400°. Arrange the slices of bread on a baking sheet and toast them in the oven for about 15 minutes, until golden brown. You want the exterior crispy, but the interior should stay soft.

Cool the bread for 2 or 3 minutes. When the bread is still slightly warm, spread a thick layer of cider jelly over each slice.

Stir the mascarpone slightly, to smooth it out, then spread a thick layer of it over the jelly. Arrange a row of peach slices over the top then sprinkle sparingly with nutmeg. Place the crostini on individual serving plates, and serve with fork and knife.

# Sweet Ricotta and
# Fresh Fruit Toasts

*Makes 4 to 6 servings*

There's something quite fun and friendly about this, a big tray of fresh sweet toasts, honey-sweetened ricotta cheese, and fresh summer fruit. You just bring everything to the table on separate plates and let everyone assemble their own open-face fruit sandwiches—which is essentially what these are. This is a dessert to be savored in July or August, when the fruit is at its peak and the setting is casual. Serve with glasses of port.

1 pound ricotta cheese
$^1/_4$ cup mild honey, like orange blossom or clover
1 tablespoon fresh lemon juice
grated zest of $^1/_2$ lemon
a drop or 2 of vanilla extract
1 long loaf French bread (baguette)
2 tablespoons unsalted butter, softened
sugar
assorted fresh summer fruit, including ripe raspberries,
    strawberries, peaches, and nectarines

In a bowl, combine the ricotta cheese, honey, lemon juice and zest, and vanilla. Stir to blend, then cover and refrigerate.

Preheat the oven to 400°. Cut the bread on the diagonal into 10 to 12 full slices, each about 1 inch thick. Butter both sides with the soft butter then lay them on a large baking sheet. Sprinkle the tops with a little sugar then toast in the oven for 15 minutes or so, until golden brown.

While the bread toasts, clean and/or slice the fruit and arrange it in bowls or on a platter. Peel peaches and nectarines, but don't slice them until the last minute. Rinse strawberries, slicing them if necessary. Don't run water over raspberries or they'll get sodden.

To serve, bring everything to the table and let each person assemble their own: Spread the sweetened ricotta thickly over the bread, and arrange the fruit on top. If the fruit isn't perfectly ripe, provide a bit of sugar on the side to sprinkle on top, and lemon slices to squeeze on the fruit as well.

# Grape and Fig Focaccia

*Makes 6 servings*

I like the idea of a grape focaccia, but in practice I've always found them disappointing: The grapes get mushy in the cooking, and when all is said and done they don't look all that appetizing either. With those thoughts in mind, I began to play around with the idea of the bread base baked alone, then topped with a fresh grape and fig compote just before serving. Now this is much more like it. The fruit is cool, fresh, and refreshing, the bread is warm and crisp—a deliciously playful contrast. And the bread acts as a convenient little sponge for any juice that runs off the fruit. These are wonderful after a light Italian meal (is there such a thing?), or a big summer salad.

1 recipe Grape and Fig Compote Perfumed with Bay Leaf
(page 148), cold

## DOUGH

1¹/₂ cups lukewarm water
one ¹/₄-ounce package (about 1 scant tablespoon) active
  dry yeast
2 tablespoons yellow cornmeal
1¹/₂ tablespoons sugar, plus another tablespoon to sprinkle
  on the dough
1¹/₂ teaspoons salt
¹/₂ cup (approximately) olive oil
¹/₂ cup whole wheat flour
3 cups unbleached all-purpose flour

If you haven't already, make the compote. Pour the water into a mixing bowl and sprinkle the yeast over it. Stir in the cornmeal, 1¹/₂ tablespoons of sugar, the salt, 2 tablespoons of the olive oil, and the whole wheat flour. Stir in 2 cups of the unbleached flour and beat vigorously with a wooden spoon for about 100 strokes. Let the dough rest for 10 minutes.

Gradually add enough of the remaining unbleached flour to make a soft, kneadable dough. Turn the dough out onto a floured surface and knead for 7 minutes, adding flour as necessary to keep the dough from sticking. Place the dough in an oiled bowl, cover, and let rise in a warm, draft-free spot until doubled in bulk, about 1 to 1 1/2 hours.

Punch the dough down and turn it out onto a floured surface. Knead briefly, then divide the dough into 6 equal pieces. Shape each piece into a ball and let rest, loosely covered with plastic wrap, for 10 minutes.

Preheat the oven to 400°. Lightly oil 2 large baking sheets.

Flour the balls lightly then pat and gently stretch them into 6-inch circles. Place 3 on each sheet, leaving plenty of space between them. Pour about 1 tablespoon of olive oil into the center of each one and brush the entire surface with it. Sprinkle the top of each circle with about 1/2 teaspoon of sugar.

Bake the breads for 20 to 25 minutes, until golden brown. Transfer the breads to a rack.

Drain some of the juice off the compote if there is a lot of it. Divide it between several serving bowls and let each person spoon the fruit over their focaccia at the table.

# Apple Apricot Strudel

*Makes 6 servings*

Making genuine strudel dough takes more time and patience than any of us seem to have. The good news is that packaged phyllo dough makes an excellent substitute. Here we stack buttered sheets of phyllo, dusting them with graham cracker crumbs, and fill the dough with chopped apples, brown sugar, golden raisins, and apricot jam; it bakes up to a golden brown and tastes smashing, alone or with a scoop of vanilla ice cream on the side.

4 graham crackers
1 tablespoon granulated sugar
2 large Golden Delicious apples, peeled, cored, and chopped into 1/2-inch chunks
1/2 cup golden raisins
1/2 cup coarsely chopped walnuts, toasted or not
1/4 cup packed light brown sugar
1/2 teaspoon ground cinnamon
6 sheets of packaged phyllo dough, measuring 14 by 18 inches

$^1/_4$ cup ($^1/_2$ stick) unsalted butter, melted
$^1/_4$ cup apricot preserves
confectioners' sugar to sift over the top

Put the graham crackers and granulated sugar in the bowl of a food processor and chop them into very fine crumbs. Transfer to a small bowl and set aside.

Preheat the oven to 375°. Lightly butter a baking sheet.

In a bowl, mix the apples, raisins, walnuts, brown sugar, and cinnamon. Mix in 1$^1/_2$ tablespoons of the ground cracker crumbs. Set aside.

Stack the 6 sheets of phyllo dough on your work counter. Directly in front of you, place 2 overlapping sheets of wax paper, several inches longer and wider than the phyllo; one of the long edges should be directly in front of you. Take one sheet of phyllo off the pile and place it in front of you on the wax paper, long edge toward you. Brush the phyllo thoroughly with melted butter and sprinkle lightly with some of the crumbs. Put another sheet directly on top of the first and do the same. Repeat for the remaining sheets, buttering and dusting with crumbs.

Visually divide your dough lengthwise into 4 equal strips. Place the apple filling in the third strip away from you, leaving a border of about 3 inches on both short sides. Dot the top of the filling with the apricot jam. Fold the short sides over the filling, then fold the top strip over the filling. (You will find it easiest to roll if you lift on the wax paper, instead of handling the strudel directly.) Continue to roll the dough the long way, toward you, until the strudel is closed.

Place the strudel on the baking sheet, seam side down. Cut 3 steam vents through the top of the dough with a sharp paring knife. Bake for 40 minutes, until golden brown.

Cool the strudel on the sheet, on a rack, for at least 10 minutes. Then slice the strudel on a slight diagonal, dust the top with confectioners' sugar, and serve.

# More Strudels to Ponder

Frozen, thawed phyllo dough can't be refrozen without becoming crumbly, or stuck, and all but impossible to handle. That gives you about a month to try your hand at yet another sweet strudel or two. Keeping in mind that you will need about 3 cups of fruit, sweetened to taste and thickened with a tablespoon or two of flour or tapioca if the fruit is juicy, consider the following:

*Apple Cranberry:* Perfect for fall. Add a bit of ground cinnamon or cardamom and cut back on the fruit if you want to add some finely chopped nuts.

*Pear Strudel:* Alone, with a tablespoon of chopped candied ginger, or slivers of dried figs.

*Berry Strudel:* Come summer, use fresh blue, black, or raspberries, alone or in combination.

*Peach Strudel:* Season with ground nutmeg and a sprinkle of almond extract.

*Or Instead of Strudel . . .*

—*To make pies and tarts,* layer 8 pieces of phyllo, lightly buttered and sprinkled with crumbs, in a pie or tart pan. You can trim the pieces to fit, like a pie shell, or offset the pieces and pull the edges up over the filling. Bake as usual.

—*To make turnovers,* place a sheet of phyllo on the work counter in front of you, short edge facing you. Butter and sprinkle with crumbs. Starting with a long edge, fold it over the center third, as though you were folding a business letter. Butter the top of the center strip. Put about 2 to 3 tablespoons of filling on top of the center strip, about 1 inch in from the short edge. Fold the other third of the phyllo over the center strip, covering the filling. Fold the strip up like a flag; fold the short edge over diagonally to meet the long edge of the "letter." Continue in this fashion to make a triangular package, then bake at 375° on a buttered sheet for about 25 to 30 minutes.

# Phyllophobic Considerations

I would like a word with all of you who suffer from phyllophobia, an affliction in search of a support group. Phyllophobia is the fear of opening a box of phyllo dough, because you darn well know the individual leaves will be laminated together in the most unfortunate places, leaving you with a gazillion shreds of useless phyllo. My advice: Take the box back for a full refund. Keep trying brands until you find one more reliable.

Or perhaps you're one of those phyllophobes who never get beyond the text of a recipe that reads: Keep the sheets covered at all times with plastic wrap and a damp towel. I used to do this; I'd make baklava, and 24 times I'd pull off the towel, the plastic, the phyllo, and replace the plastic, then the towel. This is no way to cook!

The fact is, if packaged phyllo is prestuck, you can keep it covered till the cows come home and it won't make one whit of difference. And if it isn't stuck together, this business of covering it every few seconds is for the severely obsessive only; I can't see that it makes any difference at all. Now, I don't recommend leaving phyllo uncovered indefinitely; if you get tied up on the phone, or otherwise distracted for several minutes, then cover it. But don't sweat it otherwise (drips of perspiration will make phyllo stick). Seldom will you use a whole box of phyllo at a time. And since I've never had much luck storing it for too long in the fridge, or refreezing it, I try to plan a series of desserts and main courses around an open box. If you want to make baklava, how about throwing together a casserole of spanakopita the same week? Or making a vegetable strudel or some dessert purses, or Sweet Phyllo Baskets (page 108)?

# Sweet Phyllo Baskets

*Makes 4 servings*

These crisp casings have so many dessert uses, and they're so quick to make, that you'll want to serve them again and again. Basically you just layer buttered phyllo sheets in custard cups, sprinkling each layer with a little sugar. Then just bake. They can act as containers for fruit compotes, sautéed apples or pears in the fall, and for whipped cream and fresh summer berries. They can also hold little scoops of sorbets and ice creams, or ice cream, sliced bananas, and chocolate sauce. You get the idea. It's best to form these using ramekins or custard cups with flat bottoms, so that the baskets can sit flat on their own. Note that you can easily multiply the number of baskets by using one extra full sheet of phyllo per person. Have everything set up and ready to assemble the baskets before you take the phyllo out of the package; if you work quickly you won't have to cover the sheets of phyllo as you go, which can be a real pain.

$1/4$ **cup granulated sugar**
**2 tablespoons unsalted butter**
**4 sheets of packaged phyllo dough, measuring 14 by 18 inches**
**confectioners' sugar for dusting (optional)**

Preheat the oven to 350°. Lightly butter four $1/2$-cup ramekins or custard cups and sprinkle each with a little of the sugar.

Melt the butter in a small saucepan. Get out a pastry brush.

Lay the sheets of phyllo on top of one another then cut them in half lengthwise, then widthwise. Stack the 4 piles on top of one another, then trim a little off one edge so the pieces are more or less square.

Brush the top square of phyllo with butter and sprinkle with a little sugar. Tuck the sheet into one of the ramekins or cups, carefully pushing the phyllo into the bottom crease. Butter and sugar another piece and tuck it in on top of the first. Do 4 sheets like this per cup, offsetting the corners slightly as you go, which will give the tops of the baskets a flower-blossom look.

Put the cups on a baking sheet and bake for 25 minutes, until golden brown. Cool for a couple of minutes in the cups, then very carefully lift the baskets out. Finish cooling on a rack. A little confectioners' sugar sieved over the upper leaves of the baskets looks very pretty.

# Crust Required:
## Perfect Pies and Tarts

If you haven't experienced the pleasure of homemade pies yourself, or have fallen out of the habit, I hope you'll flip through this chapter and find the necessary inspiration to get up and running. Pies and tarts are actually simple to make, so long as you heed some very basic pointers (see page 130). I know making pastry gives some would-be pie bakers the heebie-jeebies, but take heart: I think I've gotten the perfect crust down to a simple science that will solve your pastry problems.

Since the pastry is the most time-consuming part of making pies, consider making several crusts at the same time and freezing them. I don't recommend doubling the recipe, since it mixes best as a single batch, but making several batches still saves you the extra time of getting out ingredients, putting them away, and cleaning up after yourself. And with frozen crusts on hand, you can put together a pie in just a few minutes. Buy some used pie pans at a yard sale, or a stack of the disposable aluminum kind at the grocery store. Freeze the unbaked pie shells separately, then once they're firm, stack them on top of one another with a piece of wax paper in between. Bag and freeze.

Not all tarts are made in a tart pan. In this chapter you'll find several pan-less sweet tarts known as crostate. Italians make crostate with ricotta cheese or fruit, among other things; you'll find three examples here of the latter. I think they're especially good for beginners because you end up with all the goodness of a tart, but miss the sometimes tricky step of getting the pastry into the tart pan. As you become more comfortable working with pastry, you can work up to tarts in the pan. And believe me, the two chocolate tarts here are worth working up to.

I tend to go in streaks when it comes to making pies and tarts; there's a natural rhythm to the pie baker's season, and I've known others who feel the same ebb and flow of inspiration that I do. It starts with the colorful fresh bounty of summer fruit, gains momentum for the arrival of fall apples and pears, then tapers off closer to the holidays when other kinds of baking vie for our time. Winter brings with it a more measured pace, and before long the cycle begins again. But no matter what the season, making simple pies and tarts is a satisfying task any of us can master.

# Peach Blueberry Pie with Almond Crumb Topping

*Makes 8 servings*

I'm a serious peach eater. For one period of my life I used to travel often between New Jersey and Virginia Beach, a trip with dozens of peach stands along the highway. I'd load up the trunk with bushel baskets full of peaches nearly the size of softballs, then go peach crazy for a week. Where we live in New Hampshire, finding a good peach can be quite difficult, so my sister Joanne—bless her—sends them up by UPS from her home in North Carolina. Since she goes to so much trouble to secure good peaches, I'm careful about how I spend my hard-earned currency, and I consider this pie one of my best investments. Peaches are the main attraction, but there are just enough blueberries in the pie to give a shot of blue here and there, a little berry flavor with every other mouthful. I like the way this toasted almond topping complements the peaches. But if toasting almonds seems like a hassle, just use the basic topping for the Apple and Cherry Crisp (page 65).

one 9-inch pie shell (page 130)

FILLING

5 cups peeled and sliced ripe peaches
1 cup blueberries
$^1/_2$ cup granulated sugar
3 tablespoons unbleached all-purpose flour
$^1/_2$ teaspoon ground nutmeg
juice of $^1/_2$ lemon
finely grated zest of 1 lemon

TOPPING

1 cup toasted almonds, cooled (page 20)
$^2/_3$ cup unbleached all-purpose flour
$^1/_2$ cup packed light brown sugar
$^1/_8$ teaspoon salt
6 tablespoons cold unsalted butter, cut into $^1/_4$-inch pieces

Prepare the pie shell and refrigerate for at least 20 minutes. Preheat the oven to 425°.

In a large bowl, toss together all of the filling ingredients. Scrape the filling into the chilled shell. Bake for 30 minutes.

As the pie bakes, prepare the topping. Put the cooled almonds in a food processor and chop them coarsely. Add the flour, brown sugar, and salt and process for 5 more seconds. Stop the machine, add the butter, then process for up to 10 more seconds, to make damp crumbs; don't overprocess or you'll turn the mixture to mush. Refrigerate the topping until ready to use.

Get out a large baking sheet and put it on top of the stove. After the initial 30 minutes of baking, put the pie on the sheet and spread the topping over the fruit. Lower the heat to 375° then bake the pie on the sheet for another 30 to 40 minutes, until bubbly.

Cool the pie on a rack for at least 30 minutes before slicing.

# Strawberry Yogurt Pie

*Makes 8 servings*

Creamy yogurt cheese—yogurt minus the whey—makes a smooth base for this seasonal, no-bake fruit pie. There are two ways to do this: Just plop the strawberries on top of the yogurt, or fancy them up with a slightly thickened strawberry puree. The fancy version takes only a few extra minutes and an extra pint of berries, but the pie is still wonderful without this touch. If the basic idea appeals to you, try this with fresh peaches too, or another berry. You can also flip the construction upside down if you like, and pour the cooled strawberry puree over the yogurt then put your choice of fruit over it instead of under it. You have to start the yogurt the day before you plan to serve the pie, so the whey will have time to drain.

1 quart plain yogurt
$^1/_4$ cup sugar
$^1/_2$ teaspoon vanilla extract
$^1/_4$ teaspoon lemon extract (optional)
one 9-inch Cinnamon Graham Cracker Crust pie shell
   (page 132), prebaked
1 quart (approximately) ripe strawberries, rinsed, hulled,
   and patted dry with paper towels

## STRAWBERRY GLAZE (OPTIONAL)

1 pint ripe strawberries, rinsed, hulled, and patted dry
$^1/_4$ cup sugar
1 tablespoon cornstarch
juice of $^1/_2$ lemon

One day ahead, line a colander with dampened cheesecloth and put the colander in a bowl. Pour the yogurt into the colander and cover it with plastic wrap. Refrigerate overnight. The next day, empty the drained yogurt into a bowl and whisk in the sugar, the vanilla extract, and lemon extract if you are using it. Scrape the filling into the pie shell and smooth it out.

Select about a quart of berries roughly the same size and arrange them over the yogurt, hulled side down. You can serve the pie just as is, but it's best if you can first refrigerate the pie, covered, for several hours.

If you want to make the optional strawberry glaze, puree the berries in a food processor. Pour the puree into a small nonreactive saucepan and whisk in the sugar and cornstarch. Bring to a boil over medium heat and boil, whisking occasionally, for 1 minute. Pour the puree into a bowl, stir in the lemon juice, and cool to lukewarm. Spoon the lukewarm puree over the top of the pie, covering all the berries. Cover with a foil tent and refrigerate for at least a couple of hours before serving.

# Blueberry Sour Cream Pie

*Makes 8 servings*

Here's a versatile pie I make with frozen blueberries, though fresh ones would work beautifully, of course. And it's even better the next day, if you can wait that long. This isn't baked. Instead, the blueberries are cooked in a saucepan and thickened with a little cornstarch. After the filling has cooled, it's topped with a combination of sour cream and cream cheese, whipped with a bit of sugar. Just chill for several hours, so the topping firms, then serve. If you have extra fresh berries around, stir a handful into the blueberry filling before it goes into the shell; the different textures are nice together. I use a graham cracker crust here, but any prebaked 9-inch pie pastry will do.

1 recipe Cinnamon Graham Cracker Crust (page 132)
one 12-ounce bag (about 2$^1$/$_2$ cups) frozen blueberries
juice of $^1$/$_2$ lemon
1 tablespoon minced candied ginger (optional)
$^1$/$_3$ cup granulated sugar
2 tablespoons cornstarch

TOPPING

4 ounces cream cheese, softened
1$^1$/$_4$ cups sour cream, at room temperature
$^1$/$_3$ cup confectioners' sugar
grated zest of 1 lemon
1 tablespoon fresh lemon juice

If you haven't already, prepare the crust. Put the blueberries, lemon juice, and ginger in a medium-size nonreactive saucepan. Cover and cook over low heat until the berries give off a fair amount of liquid, about 5 minutes.

In a small bowl, mix the granulated sugar and cornstarch. Turn the heat up to medium and add the sugar-cornstarch mixture. Bring the berries to a boil, stirring, and boil for 1$^1$/$_2$ minutes. Scrape the filling onto a plate and cool to lukewarm. Spoon the filling into the pastry and refrigerate, uncovered, for an hour.

In a bowl, beat the cream cheese with an electric mixer or by hand, to make it fluffy. Add the remaining topping ingredients and beat until smooth. Spoon the topping over the filling then smooth it out with a spoon. Cover with tented foil and refrigerate for at least 3 hours before slicing, though overnight is better.

# Chocolate Pecan Pie

*Makes 8 servings*

Food writers constantly think about improving on the tried and true, a habit that breeds both genius and folly. When I began thinking about "improving" gooey pecan pie, the best I could come up with was chocolate. The result was immensely gratifying, perhaps improved from a chocoholic's perspective, but actually in a class of its own. The filling, especially at the center, has the near-gooey texture we all love in pecan pie. And the surface has a gorgeous finish of glazed pecans. As you can tell, I'm crazy about this pie and I think you'll feel the same. Serve with whipped cream, vanilla or chocolate ice cream.

Try to make this pie a day ahead for best texture.

**one 9-inch unbaked pie shell (page 130)**

### FILLING

$^1/_2$ **cup honey**
$^1/_2$ **cup packed light brown sugar**
$^1/_4$ **cup ($^1/_2$ stick) unsalted butter, cut into several large pieces**
**4 ounces semisweet chocolate, coarsely chopped**
**big pinch of salt**
**3 large eggs, plus 1 egg yolk**
**2 teaspoons vanilla extract**
**1$^1/_2$ cups coarsely chopped toasted pecans (page 20)**

Chill the pie shell for at least 30 minutes. Preheat the oven to 350°.
Put the honey and brown sugar in a small saucepan and bring to a boil over

medium heat. Reduce the heat slightly and simmer, stirring, for 1 minute. Turn the heat off and add the butter and chocolate. Let sit for 10 minutes, then whisk to smooth. Scrape the contents of the pan into a bowl and cool for 10 minutes.

Whisk the salt, eggs, yolk, and vanilla extract in a separate bowl, then whisk them into the chocolate mixture until smooth. Stir in the chopped pecans. Scrape the filling into the chilled pie shell.

Bake the pie for 40 to 50 minutes. When done, the pie will puff but may still seem slightly wobbly in the center; that's good. Cool the pie on a rack. The texture improves markedly as the pie sits; several hours is good, but overnight—covered and refrigerated—is best.

# Brandied Dried Fruit and Apple Pie

*Makes 8 servings*

I think making a good apple pie is one of the kindest things you can do for yourself or a friend. When I was a kid, my dad used to make wonderful apple pies, and they still give me warm family feelings to this day. Here's an adult apple pie, made with dried fruit soaked in brandy; if you haven't any dried fruit on hand, you can substitute $^1/_3$ cup brandy plus $^1/_4$ cup each of raisins and chopped pitted prunes. As you'd expect, the brandy gives the pie an agreeable little kick. Serve the pie still warm, and you'll have rivulets of apple-brandy juice that simply cry out for vanilla ice cream.

one unbaked 9-inch pie shell (page 130), chilled

FILLING

6 large Golden Delicious apples, peeled, cored, and sliced
$^1/_2$ cup sugar
1 tablespoon fresh lemon juice
$^1/_3$ cup brandy *plus* $^1/_2$ cup Dried Fruit in Brandy (page 166)
2 tablespoons flour
$^1/_2$ teaspoon ground cinnamon

---

*Crust Required* 115

TOPPING

1 cup unbleached all-purpose flour
$^1/_2$ cup sugar
pinch of salt
$^1/_2$ cup (1 stick) cold unsalted butter, cut into $^1/_2$-inch
  pieces

Chill the pie shell for at least 30 minutes. Preheat the oven to 425°.

Toss together all the filling ingredients and set aside for 10 minutes. Toss again, then turn the filling into the shell and shape the top into an even dome with your hands.

Place the pie on a baking sheet and put it in the oven. Cover the pie loosely with a piece of tented aluminum foil and bake for 45 minutes.

Put the flour, sugar, and salt in a food processor. Process for 5 seconds. Add the butter and process for about 10 to 15 seconds, just until the mixture shows signs of forming clumps. Transfer to a bowl and rub the topping several times between your fingers to even it out.

After 45 minutes, slide the pie out and uncover. Cover the pie with the topping, patting it on gently. Reduce the heat to 350° and bake, uncovered, for another 35 to 45 minutes, until good and bubbly.

Cool the pie on a rack for at least 30 minutes before slicing. This is best eaten warm or at room temperature.

# Creamy Pumpkin Pie

*Makes 8 servings*

This is less like any pumpkin pie you've probably ever had, and more like pumpkin cheesecake. But don't worry, you won't be disappointed! My son Ben who loves pumpkin anything, says this is the best pumpkin pie in the world. I rest my case. Because this is so similar to cheesecake, you could in fact bake it in an 8-inch springform pan for approximately the same amount of time. If you like a spicy pie, use a little bit more of each spice than I call for—the seasoning here is mild.

one 9-inch Cinnamon Graham Cracker Crust pie shell
   (page 132), prebaked

FILLING

8 ounces cream cheese, softened to room temperature
2/3 cup packed light brown sugar
1 large egg, plus 1 egg yolk
1 teaspoon vanilla extract
1 tablespoon unbleached all-purpose flour
1/2 teaspoon *each* ground cinnamon, ground ginger, and
   ground nutmeg
3/4 cup canned pumpkin
1/3 cup heavy cream

Let the pie shell cool after baking. Preheat the oven to 350°.

In a bowl, beat the cream cheese and brown sugar with an electric mixer or by hand until soft and fluffy. Beat in the egg, yolk, and vanilla. Mix the flour and spices and beat them in also. Add the pumpkin and cream and blend until the filling is uniform, scraping down the sides of the bowl.

Pour the filling into the crust and bake for 45 to 50 minutes; when the pie is done, the center may seem a bit wobbly, but it shouldn't be liquidy-loose.

Cool the pie on a rack, then cover and refrigerate for at least 4 hours before serving.


# *Apple Pie in Orange Custard*

*Makes 8 servings*

If you love custard, and apple pie—and who doesn't?—you can imagine what a blissful state this custard apple pie induces. The custard settles in and around the sautéed slices of Golden Delicious apples, leaving them soft and fragrant with the scent of orange. This needs no accompaniment but fresh coffee and perhaps a dollop of whipped cream or lightly sweetened sour cream. Make the pastry and get it into the pan the day ahead, and this will come together quickly.

# CUSTARD

$^3/_4$ cup milk
$^1/_3$ cup sugar
3 egg yolks
1 teaspoon orange extract, *or* $^1/_2$ teaspoon vanilla extract
  plus the grated zest of $^1/_2$ orange
one unbaked 9-inch pie shell (page 130)

## APPLE FILLING

2 tablespoons unsalted butter
6 large Golden Delicious apples, peeled, cored, and sliced
$^1/_4$ cup plus 2 tablespoons sugar
1 tablespoon flour

Heat the milk and sugar in a small saucepan, stirring to dissolve the sugar. Remove from the heat and cool for 5 minutes.

Whisk the egg yolks in a small bowl, gradually adding the warm milk. Stir in the flavoring.

Partially prebake the crust. At the end of the baking time, ladle about 2 or 3 tablespoons of custard over the bottom of the crust, just enough to cover. Bake for 5 more minutes then transfer to a rack and cool.

Melt the butter in a large, heavy skillet. Stir in the apple slices and sauté over medium-high heat for 3 minutes. Sprinkle on $^1/_4$ cup of the sugar and sauté for another 3 or 4 minutes, until the slices are almost tender. Remove from the heat, stir in the flour, and cool to room temperature.

Gently scrape the apple slices into the pan and even the top. Ladle the rest of the custard over the apples; it should not come closer than $^1/_4$ inch to the rim. Sprinkle the remaining 2 tablespoons of sugar over the pie.

Bake the pie for 40 minutes, until the custard is fairly well set; a few pockets of wobbly custard are fine because they'll firm as the pie cools. Serve warm or at room temperature. Once cool, cover and refrigerate right away.

# Fig Pie

*Makes 8 servings*

This is my answer to always feeling cheated on the fig filling in fig cookies. First I simmer dried figs in pear juice, which you can find at any health food store; I use After The Fall brand juice, made in Vermont. Then I simply puree the figs with a little sugar, vanilla, citrus zest, and eggs. It makes an incredibly fragrant, light filling, with a texture not unlike pumpkin pie. Serve with coffee or vanilla ice cream.

one 9-inch pie shell (page 130), prebaked

FILLING

$^1/_2$ pound dried figs, halved and stems removed
$2^1/_2$ cups pear juice
$^3/_4$ cup walnut pieces
$^1/_2$ cup sugar
2 large eggs
2 teaspoons vanilla extract
1 tablespoon fresh lemon juice
finely grated zest of 1 lemon and 1 orange

Cool the pie shell if you haven't already.

Combine the figs and pear juice in a medium-size nonreactive saucepan. Bring to a simmer, then cover and cook the figs at an active simmer for 40 minutes, until very soft. Transfer them to a bowl and cool to room temperature. Set the oven at 375°.

Put the walnuts in the bowl of a food processor and process until finely chopped. Transfer the nuts to a bowl. After the nuts are chopped, puree the figs and their juice and the sugar until smooth. Add the remaining ingredients—except the nuts—and puree again until smooth, about 5 seconds. Transfer the puree to the bowl with the nuts and stir to blend.

Scrape the filling into the shell and bake the pie for 20 minutes, then reduce the heat to 350° and bake for another 45 minutes; when done, the pie should puff slightly and have fissures around the outside. Cool on a rack and serve warm or at room temperature.

# Blueberry Pear Pie

*Makes 8 servings*

Winter is too long here in New Hampshire, and summer too short, to overlook frozen berries when you need a hold-you-over fruit pie right now. I buy bags of wild Maine IQF blueberries (that's individually quick-frozen) and they're just fine. Combined with sliced pears, they make one impressive fruit pie for a cold winter's night or when cabin fever really strikes. The filling needs just a bit of sugar and spice, a touch of lemon, and an oat-crumb topping, and you're in business. Go all out, and serve à la mode.

one 9-inch unbaked pie shell (page 130), chilled

FILLING

one 12-ounce bag (about 2$^1$/$_2$ cups) frozen wild
   blueberries
3 large ripe pears, peeled, cored, and sliced
$^1$/$_2$ cup granulated sugar
2 tablespoons unbleached all-purpose flour
1 teaspoon ground cinnamon
1 tablespoon fresh lemon juice

TOPPING

$^1$/$_2$ cup unbleached all-purpose flour
$^1$/$_3$ cup packed light brown sugar
$^1$/$_4$ cup rolled oats
$^1$/$_2$ teaspoon ground cinnamon
pinch of salt
$^1$/$_4$ cup ($^1$/$_2$ stick) cold unsalted butter, cut into $^1$/$_4$-inch
   pieces

While the pie shell chills, preheat the oven to 425°.

To make the filling, combine all the ingredients in a mixing bowl. Toss well. Scrape the filling into the chilled shell and put the pie on a baking sheet. Bake for 30 minutes.

While the pie is baking, put the topping ingredients in a bowl and rub them together until you have gravelly crumbs. Cover and refrigerate.

After 30 minutes, slide the pie out of the oven on its baking sheet. Cover the pie evenly with the crumbs, then reduce the oven heat to 375° and bake for another 45 minutes or so, until the juice is bubbly and the topping is golden brown. Slide the pie onto a rack and cool to lukewarm or room temperature before slicing.

# Sour Cream Raisin Pie

*Makes 8 servings*

Everybody needs at least a couple of pies you can throw together in seconds; this is a good one. Just buzz all the filling ingredients in a food processor, pour into the pie shell, and bake. This is a custard pie, with a slight sour cream tang balanced by the addition of raisins. Like all custard pies, it can't be baked too quickly or you'll ruin the otherwise silken texture. Plan to let this cool for at least 1 hour before serving, though I much prefer it chilled.

**one 9-inch pie shell (page 130), prebaked and cooled**

## FILLING

$1^1/_2$ cups sour cream, at room temperature
1 (scant) cup sugar
3 large eggs, at room temperature
2 tablespoons unsalted butter, softened to room
 temperature
$1^1/_2$ teaspoons vanilla extract
finely grated zest of 1 lemon
2 tablespoons unbleached all-purpose flour
$^1/_2$ cup raisins

While the pie shell cools, set the oven at 350°.

In the bowl of a food processor, put the sour cream, sugar, eggs, butter, vanilla, and lemon zest. Puree for about 10 seconds, until uniformly smooth. Scrape down the sides, add the flour, and process for another 5 seconds.

Scatter the raisins in the bottom of the pastry. Slowly pour the filling into the shell, then bake the pie for 40 to 45 minutes. When done, the sides of the pie will puff slightly and the center will still be jiggly, though not liquidy-loose.

Cool the pie on a rack for at least 1 hour before serving. If you're not serving it right away, cool the pie to room temperature, cover loosely with foil, and refrigerate. It will keep for a couple of days in good condition.

# Toasted Coconut Mocha Mud Pie

*Makes 6 to 8 servings*

This belongs in the Dessert Hall of Fame, not least because the end product is so wildly, disproportionately good for the amount of work involved. True, there are several elements here, but each one is an utter snap to make; if need be, you can also fall back on a store-bought graham cracker crust. You can add your personal signature by using a favorite ice cream; Ben & Jerry's makes a White Russian that's great, with the chocolate sauce and toasted coconut. This takes a little longer than you'd like to reharden in the freezer to the proper slicing texture, but be patient or it will slop all over the plates. The best way to approach this is to get the ice cream in the crust, then start the sauce.

> one 9-inch Cinnamon Graham Cracker Crust (page 132),
>   prebaked
> 1 pint good-quality coffee ice cream
> 1 recipe 5-Minute Chocolate Sauce (page 198)
> 1 cup unsweetened shredded coconut (available at health
>   food stores) or flaked sweetened coconut

While the crust cools, slightly soften the ice cream in the refrigerator.

Spoon the ice cream into a bowl and work it with a wooden spoon until it is pliable but not too soft. Scrape it into the cooled crust and spread it evenly. Put the pie in the freezer.

Prepare the sauce if you haven't already. When it has cooled to room temperature but is still pourable, slowly pour all of it over the ice cream and tilt the pie so the chocolate runs up to the crust. Put the pie back in the freezer.

Put the coconut in a skillet and turn the heat on low. Toast the coconut for 2 to 5 minutes, until golden brown, stirring almost constantly. Immediately dump the coconut onto a plate and cool.

Sprinkle the coconut evenly over the chocolate. Cover the pie loosely with foil and freeze for at least 3 hours, or until the ice cream is firm. Slice and serve.

# *Chocolate Almond Tart*

*Makes 8 to 10 servings*

This dense, dusky chocolate tart has a crunchy top and moist interior. It tastes heavenly, and you'll appreciate having no chocolate to melt; you just chop it up with the nuts. The addition of a little extra cocoa gives the tart a smooth, almost velvety texture and a deeper chocolate flavor. Serve with scoops of good coffee ice cream.

**one 9-inch tart shell (page 130), prebaked and cooled**

FILLING

1 cup toasted whole almonds, cooled (page 20)
5 ounces semisweet chocolate, coarsely chopped
2 tablespoons plus $^1/_3$ cup sugar
3 tablespoons unsweetened cocoa powder
2 large eggs, at room temperature, plus 1 egg yolk
2 tablespoons dark rum or bourbon
1 teaspoon vanilla extract
2 tablespoons unsalted butter, melted

While the tart shell cools, preheat the oven to 350°.

Put $^1/_2$ cup of the almonds into a food processor with the chocolate and 2 tablespoons of the sugar. Process to a fine consistency, then add the cocoa and process for a few more seconds. Set aside.

In a bowl, using an electric mixer, beat the eggs, yolk, and remaining $^1/_3$ cup of sugar on high speed until doubled in volume, about $1^1/_2$ minutes. Blend in the rum or bourbon and vanilla, then fold in the dry mixture. Fold in the butter until smooth.

Coarsely chop the remaining almonds and fold them into the batter. Scrape the batter into the shell. Bake the tart for 30 minutes; when done, the edge will be slightly puffed and the center barely set. Cool on a rack. Serve warm or at room temperature.

# Chocolate and Walnut Fudge Tart

*Makes 10 servings*

Are you one of those chocolate fiends who eats fudge sauce cold, straight from the jar, when nobody else is looking? That's just what this tart is all about: a fudge sauce poured into a prebaked tart shell. You have two options here: Strew the chopped nuts directly over the chocolate as it begins to set. Or spread the optional sour cream layer over the chocolate and *then* put down the nuts (decisions, decisions!). The beauty of the lightly sweetened sour cream layer is that it gives a tang as well as contrasting color to the sweet chocolate; the beauty of leaving it out is fewer calories, and a tad less work. Your call.

one 9-inch tart shell (page 130), prebaked and cooled

### FILLING AND NUTS

12 ounces semisweet chocolate, coarsely chopped
1 cup heavy cream
$^1/_4$ cup coffee liqueur
2 teaspoons vanilla extract
$1^1/_2$ cups coarsely chopped walnuts, preferably toasted
   (page 20)

### SOUR CREAM TOPPING (OPTIONAL)

1 cup sour cream
3 tablespoons sugar

While the tart shell cools on a rack, put the chopped chocolate in a medium mixing bowl. Heat the cream almost to the boiling point, then add the coffee liqueur. Swirl the pan, heating for 5 seconds, then pour the hot liquid over the chocolate. Let the mixture sit for 5 minutes, then add the vanilla and whisk until the chocolate is smooth.

Cool the chocolate for 20 or 30 minutes, then whisk again and pour it into the cooled shell. Jiggle the shell to spread the chocolate out. Cool to room temperature.

If you're putting the nuts directly on top of the chocolate, refrigerate the tart for about 30 minutes, then sprinkle the nuts over the top. Press them down *very gently* to embed them slightly. Cover and refrigerate for at least 4 hours before serving.

If you're using the sour cream topping, cover and refrigerate the tart for at least an hour. After an hour, put the sour cream and sugar in a small nonreactive saucepan. Heat, stirring, just bringing the sour cream to about body temperature. Pour the sour cream over the center of the tart, jiggling the tart to spread it out to the crust. Cool for 5 minutes, then sprinkle the nuts evenly over the topping. Cover loosely with plastic wrap and refrigerate for at least 3 more hours before serving.

# Apple Raspberry Phyllo Tart

*Makes 5 servings*

Layered phyllo sheets serve as the foundation for this attractive tart. The top layer of phyllo is smeared with raspberry jam, then apple slices are arranged over it in short crosswise rows and brushed with more raspberry jam. The tart bakes up to a pretty pink finish, and tastes wonderful—slightly cooled—served with a scoop of whipped cream and fresh raspberries scattered over the top.

3 large apples, peeled and halved
1 tablespoon fresh lemon juice
1 tablespoon sugar
1 teaspoon ground cinnamon
3 tablespoons unsalted butter, melted
3 sheets of phyllo dough, measuring 14 by 18 inches
1/4 cup fine graham cracker crumbs
1/4 cup plus 2 tablespoons raspberry preserves
whipped cream and fresh raspberries (optional)

Carefully, so you don't split them, cut the cores out of the apples. Cut the apples into 1/4-inch-thick crosswise slices. Remove the smallest end cuts and reserve them for another use. Toss the more uniform center-cut slices in a bowl with the lemon juice and set aside.

Mix the sugar and cinnamon in a small bowl and place it near your work area. Leave the butter right in the pan you melted it in, and put it in your work area also.

Preheat the oven to 350° and butter a large cookie sheet.

Cut the phyllo dough in half lengthwise; you will have 6 pieces measuring 18 by 7 inches. Lay the first sheet on your baking sheet, centered. Brush with melted butter, then sprinkle the surface with cinnamon sugar and cracker crumbs.

Place a second sheet on top of the first, covering it with butter, sugar, and crumbs. Continue in this manner until all the sheets are stacked.

Spread 1/4 cup of the raspberry preserves over the top sheet of phyllo, leaving a 1-inch border all around.

Starting at the center of the tart, arrange a row of slightly overlapping apple slices on top of the preserves; it will take 5 or 6 slices to go across. Make 2 more rows on either side of the center row, leaving you with 5 rows.

Put the remaining 2 tablespoons of preserves in the pan with whatever butter is left. Heat the preserves to loosen them up, then brush it over the apples. Fold the uncovered edge of the dough up over the apples. Bake the tart for 40 to 45 minutes, until the edges are golden brown and the preserves are bubbling hot.

Cool the tart on the sheet for 10 minutes, then carefully use spatulas to lift or slide it directly onto a rack. Cool for at least 15 more minutes, then slice and serve with whipped cream and raspberries, if you like.

# *Sweet Cherry Crostata*

*Makes 6 to 8 servings*

A crostata is an Italian dessert tart. It can be made in a tart pan, but I like the rough-around-the-edges look of a free-form crostata. Here I use sweet dark cherries: The filling goes in the center, then the sides of the pastry are folded up over it. One common crostata mistake is not leaving a wide enough border to fold back comfortably over the filling; a generous 2 inches is about right. Even if you have to pick the cherries out of the box one by one, try to get the ripest (dark and somewhat soft) cherries you can find. Good cherries don't need too much embellishment, so I keep to the basics, with just a hint of cardamom for fun. Excellent warm, with vanilla ice cream.

1 recipe Simple Pie Pastry (page 131), chilled

## FILLING

1 quart sweet cherries, pitted and halved
juice and finely grated zest of 1 lemon
1 teaspoon vanilla extract
$^{1}/_{3}$ cup sugar
2 tablespoons unbleached all-purpose
　flour
$^{1}/_{8}$ teaspoon ground cardamom

Preheat the oven to 400°. On a sheet of lightly floured wax paper, roll the chilled pie pastry into a 13- to 14-inch circle. Invert the pastry onto a large baking sheet. Cover with plastic wrap and refrigerate.

To make the filling, in a bowl, stir the cherries, lemon juice and zest, and vanilla. Mix the remaining dry ingredients in another bowl and stir them into the fruit. Set aside.

Remove the pastry from the fridge and let it sit for 5 minutes or so, until it seems pliant enough to fold over the filling. Scrape the filling into the center of the pastry and spread it all around to within 2 inches of the border. Fold the edge of the pastry up over the filling; it will have a pleated look.

Bake the crostata for 50 minutes, until the pastry is golden and the filling bubbles. Cool on the sheet for at least 10 minutes, then slice into wedges and serve.

# *Pear Crostata with Ginger Preserves*

*Makes 6 servings*

I bake with pears all the time, probably more than I do with apples. If you share my fondness for them, here's a dessert I know you'll want to try. Like the cherry crostata, this is a free-form tart, full of chunky pears over a thin layer of ginger preserves. If you want to take a little extra time, you can give the top of the tart a flourish by arranging some of the pear slices in a circle in the center (see Note). Either way, this is a classic fall and winter dessert, great with nothing more than a cup of strong coffee. Of course, nobody would turn down a little vanilla ice cream or whipped cream on the side if you offered it.

1 recipe Simple Pie Pastry (page 131), chilled

## FILLING

$^1/_3$ cup sugar
2 tablespoons unbleached all-purpose flour
1 teaspoon ground cinnamon
4 large ripe pears, peeled, quartered, and cored
$^1/_3$ cup ginger preserves

While the pastry chills, get out a large baking sheet and preheat the oven to 425°.

In a small bowl, combine the sugar, flour, and cinnamon and set it aside.

Cut the pear quarters crosswise into short chunks about $^1/_4$ inch thick, letting them fall into a mixing bowl. Pour the sugar mixture over them and toss thoroughly.

On a sheet of lightly floured wax paper, roll the dough into a 13- to 14-inch circle. Invert the pastry onto the baking sheet. Warm the preserves to thin them out, then spread them over the pastry to within 2 inches of the border. Scrape the pears onto the pastry, spreading them evenly over the preserves.

Fold the edge of the pastry up over the filling in a pleated fashion. Bake the crostata for 20 minutes, then lower the heat to 400° and bake for another 30 minutes, until it's golden brown and bubbly.

Cool the crostata in the pan, on a rack, for 15 to 20 minutes before slicing into wedges.

*Note:* For a slightly fancier rendition, proceed like so: Reserve 3 tablespoons of the sugar mixture separate from the greater portion. Cut 2 of the pears into chunks, as described, and mix with the greater portion of the dry mix. Spread the pears on top of the preserves as before. Peel and quarter the other 2 pears, then core. Cut the quarter sections into thick lengthwise slices, as you would for a pie. Arrange the slices in a circular fashion on top of the pear chunks, like the spokes of a bicycle wheel. Sprinkle evenly with the remaining dry mixture. Fold up the sides and bake as directed.

# Banana Crostata with Walnut Topping

*Makes 8 to 10 servings*

Staple that they are, bananas deserve more attention when it comes to dessert making. Here they get their due in a free-form tart with a cakey walnut topping. The baking brings out the sweetness of the bananas, and the walnut topping—which goes on in little globs here and there—spreads to envelop all of the fruit. Serve very warm or tepid, and plan to serve the whole thing; it isn't a great keeper. Great with lightly sweetened whipped cream and fresh hot coffee.

1 recipe Simple Pie Pastry (page 131), chilled

FILLING

5 medium-size ripe bananas
2 tablespoons unsalted butter, softened
2 tablespoons granulated sugar

TOPPING

$^{1}/_{2}$ cup walnut pieces
$^{1}/_{3}$ cup unbleached all-purpose flour
$^{1}/_{3}$ cup packed light brown sugar
1 teaspoon baking powder
$^{1}/_{4}$ cup ($^{1}/_{2}$ stick) cold unsalted butter, cut into $^{1}/_{4}$-inch
    pieces
1 large egg

While the pastry chills, preheat the oven to 400°. Lightly butter a large baking sheet.

On a sheet of floured wax paper, roll the dough out into a 13-inch circle. Invert the pastry onto the baking sheet.

# A Short Course in Pastry Miracles

1. On a hot day, make pastry early in the day, or later in the evening; a hot kitchen will frustrate your efforts.

2. Use *cold* butter; get it out last, after your dry ingredients are already mixed.

3. If you're making a food processor dough, don't overprocess the pastry. Stop the machine before the pastry balls together—it should seem somewhat dry and crumbly. If you're mixing the pastry by hand, work quickly so the butter doesn't begin to melt.

4. Refrigerate your dough for about 30 to 45 minutes. This firms up the butter and gives your pastry the strength to hold together when rolled. The proper rolling texture is cold-firm, yet malleable.

5. Roll on a sheet of wax paper, right to the edge for a pastry that will fit perfectly in a 9-inch pan. Lightly flour the pin and pastry, if necessary, to prevent sticking.

6. Flip the pastry, still on the paper, over the pan, then peel off the paper.

7. Gently nudge the pastry into the pan, without stretching it.

8. Chill your pie or tart shell for 20 to 30 minutes in the freezer before using it.

9. Exude confidence. Pastry is like the strange dog you see coming toward you; if you act scared, it will bite you.

Peel the bananas and halve them lengthwise. Starting about 2 inches in from the edge, lay the bananas flat side down on the pastry. Arrange the slices in snug concentric circles, working toward the center. Don't worry too much about symmetry, because the topping will cover your artwork.

Turn the edge of the pastry up over the bananas. Spread the soft butter over the bananas, then sprinkle them with the granulated sugar. Bake for 30 minutes while you make the topping.

Put the walnuts, flour, brown sugar, and baking powder in the bowl of a food processor and process for several seconds, until the nuts are coarsely chopped. Add the butter and process for a few more seconds, until the nuts are finely ground. Add the egg and process for 3 more seconds. Transfer the topping to a bowl and refrigerate.

When the tart has baked for 30 minutes, spoon the topping in small evenly spaced mounds over the bananas. Bake the tart for another 20 to 25 minutes, until the topping is a deep golden brown.

Partially cool the tart on a rack and serve lukewarm or at room temperature.

# Simple Pie Pastry

*Makes one 9-inch pie or tart shell*

Some may think it odd that my basic recipe for pie pastry has oats in it. It certainly isn't a traditional or classic rendition of pastry, but it works; I know because I've been making this, or some variation of it, for many years. Besides adding flavor and texture, the oats serve one very important function: They help keep the dough from shrinking or losing its shape as it so often does, especially in inexperienced hands. So this is a user-friendly pastry; if you've had trouble with other recipes, give this one a try.

$1/3$ cup rolled oats
2 tablespoons sugar
$1/8$ teaspoon salt
$1^1/4$ cups unbleached all-purpose flour
$1/2$ cup (1 stick) very cold unsalted butter, cut into $1/4$-inch
  pieces
1 egg yolk
2 to 3 tablespoons cold water

Put the oats, sugar, and salt in a food processor and process to a fine meal, 30 to 40 seconds. Add the flour and process for 5 more seconds.

Take the cover off the processor bowl and scatter the butter pieces over the dry ingredients. Process for about 8 seconds, until the butter is broken into very small pieces.

Stir the yolk and 2 tablespoons of the cold water in a small bowl. Take the lid off the machine again and sprinkle this egg water over the flour. Turn the machine on for 4 seconds, then stop it. Take the lid off, fluff up the ingredients with a fork, then re-cover and process for about 4 more seconds, until the pastry *just* starts to gather into a mass. It's okay if there are some visible dry areas.

Dump the pastry out onto your work counter and try packing it into a ball. If it doesn't pack easily, sprinkle a teaspoon of the remaining water over the dry areas and quickly work it in with your fingertips. Use even a bit more water if necessary to pack the dough into a ball. Knead it twice, then place the dough on a sheet of lightly floured wax paper. Flatten the dough into a disk about 3/4 inch thick, and refrigerate for 30 to 45 minutes. It shouldn't get rock hard.

When the dough is firm, but not too hard, roll it into a 12-inch circle on a sheet of lightly floured wax paper. Invert the pastry over a 9-inch pie pan and peel off the paper. Tuck the pastry into the pan and turn the edge under, shaping an upstanding edge. Freeze the shell for 20 minutes before using.

To bake the shell, preheat the oven to 400°. Line the shell with foil and weight it with beans, rice, or pie weights. Bake for 15 minutes, remove the foil with the weights still in it, and bake for another 7 minutes—for a partially baked shell—or about 12 minutes for a fully baked shell. (Save the weights for future shells.) If the shell starts to puff during the second part of the baking, pierce it once with a fork to let steam escape. Cool the shell on a rack.

# Cinnamon Graham Cracker Crust

*Makes enough for one 8- or*

*9-inch cheesecake or piecrust*

This is the old dependable formula I've been using for years. For best results, press it into your pan right after you make it; it holds together best when everything is newly dampened. If, however, the crust seems a tad dry and won't stay in place, sprinkle a teaspoon of water over the crust and work it in with your hands. The nut variation is what I use with the wonderful Frozen Peanut Cloud Pie on page 194.

1 package ($^1/_3$ pound) plain graham crackers
$^1/_4$ cup packed light brown sugar
$^1/_4$ teaspoon ground cinnamon
pinch of salt
5 tablespoons unsalted butter, melted

Preheat the oven to 350°. Butter an 8- or 9-inch round pan.

Break up the crackers with your hands, dropping them into the bowl of a food processor. Add the brown sugar and process to a fine meal. Pour the meal into a bowl and add the cinnamon and salt. Add the melted butter and mix—your hands work best here—to form evenly dampened crumbs.

Press the mixture into your buttered pan. Unless otherwise noted, this crust is pre-baked for 10 minutes in a preheated 350° oven.

*Variation:* Peanut or Almond Crumb Crust—Use only 9 crackers (there's usually 11 per package), granulated sugar instead of brown sugar, and $^1/_3$ cup roasted, salted peanuts. Mix as above, combining the nuts with the crackers in the food processor. For an almond crust, proceed as for the peanut crust, but use whole blanched or unblanched almonds instead.

# Fruit Finales

Americans haven't traditionally considered fruit a fitting end to the meal, perhaps partly because it's so hard to find delicious ripe fruit. Almost without exception, the best fruits I find are the ones I discover outside the mainstream of commerce—the farmstand down the road that sells local strawberries, or an out-of-the-way supplier of small, sweet New Jersey peaches, or the ones that I forage myself.

If I sometimes find the lack of exceptional fruit bothersome, it's also been instructive: The limitations have heightened my appreciation for simple fruit desserts. And I've learned to make the best of what *is* available, rather than focusing on what isn't.

The best fruit needs the least amount of tweaking to render it sublime. One important principle to remember is never to overwhelm the subtle flavor of good fruit by pairing it with too many, or overly assertive flavors. The perfect partner to fruit is one that enhances its flavor, heightens its perfume, or provides a natural contrast. Cheese and fruit are a classic example, and the right combinations can be sensational, if stunningly simple. Think of how heavenly a crisp, juicy tart apple tastes with a sharp, creamy room-temperature Cheddar. Or sweet pears with a well-aged blue cheese. This is blissful eating.

Fruit compotes capture the essence of fruit in their own very special way, by providing a liquid medium to hold flavors in. Wine is often the liquid of choice. Wine provides acidic balance and fruity emphasis, without interfering with the flavor of fruit. Compotes are often simmered to release locked-in flavors. But one of my favorite compotes is just a cornucopia of red summer fruit piled high in a goblet and covered with pink champagne.

Some firm fruits, like apples and pears, can be quickly sautéed to their advantage. These crisp fall fruits are wonderful fresh, but they're also very special when they're warm and soft, bathed in a rich creamy chocolate or caramel sauce. Time-saver that it is, the fruit sauté is a handy little item to have in your dessert repertoire.

Then there's grilled fruit, a new idea I find appealing. You'll find several of my favorite ways with grilled fruit in this chapter also.

For those of us who grew up in the American tradition of mile-high pies and triple layer cakes, warming up to the idea of fruit desserts may take some doing. But once you've gotten into the habit, you'll soon fall in love with the subtle pleasures they have to offer.

# Ruby Red Grapefruit and Cranberry Compote

*Makes 6 servings*

This is one of my favorite autumn compotes, bright red as the maple leaves on a New Hampshire hillside during fall foliage. The combination of cranberries and grapefruit is naturally tart and refreshing, best tempered and balanced with a minimum of sugar. I like it chilled and unadorned except for a garnish of mint sugar—roughly equal parts chopped fresh mint and sugar, minced together and added at the last moment. Start this the morning before you plan to serve it, so the flavors have time to blend and deepen.

> one 12-ounce bag cranberries
> 1$^1$/$_2$ cups water
> $^1$/$_2$ (scant) cup sugar
> several long strips of orange zest
> 1 cinnamon stick (optional)
> 4 large ruby red grapefruit
> mint sugar (optional—see headnote)

Put the cranberries, water, and sugar in a large nonreactive saucepan and bring to a boil. Boil, covered, for 3 minutes, then uncover and continue to boil for several more minutes, until the liquid turns syrupy; it won't take long. Remove from the heat and scrape the mixture into a bowl. Stir in the orange zest and bury the cinnamon stick in it. Leave at room temperature for an hour, stirring occasionally. Cover and refrigerate.

About an hour before serving, halve and section the grapefruits, squeezing the sections and juice right into the cranberry bowl. Stir, then cover and refrigerate until serving. Serve as is, or with the mint sugar.

---

# Fresh Berry Compote in Honey Ginger Cream

*Makes 4 servings*

The best part of summer, from this cook's point of view, is when the various berry seasons collide, leaving one gasping with pure pleasure at the possibilities. Certainly the mixed berry cobblers and pies are right at the top of my Best Desserts list, but for sheer purity and simplicity, you can't beat this. Just put your favorite summer berries in a bowl, and pour some of the ginger-infused cream over them. Don't worry about the precise proportions of berries; use whatever is available and looks good. Keep in mind that the cream needs to be prepared the evening before, or at least several hours ahead, so it has time to chill and really absorb the flavor of the ginger.

> 1 cup light cream
> $^1/_2$ cup heavy cream
> $^1/_4$ cup mild honey, such as clover
> 2 tablespoons sugar
> a big thumb-size piece of fresh ginger, peeled
> $^1/_4$ teaspoon vanilla extract
> about 4 cups (total) fresh blueberries, strawberries,
>    blackberries, and/or raspberries

In a small nonreactive saucepan, combine the creams, honey, and sugar. Cut the ginger into quarter-size slices and add them too. Heat for about 5 minutes, bringing the mixture to a near boil, stirring occasionally. Remove from the heat and stir in the vanilla extract.

Pour the liquid into a large glass measuring cup or bowl and cool to room temperature. Cover and refrigerate for at least 2 hours, or overnight.

When you are ready to serve, put about 1 cup of mixed berries into 4 dessert bowls; if you are using large strawberries, halve or quarter them first. Strain the cream through a sieve, then pour some of it over each portion. Serve right away.

# Raspberry, Grapefruit, and Melon Compote

*Makes 4 servings*

I've always loved the way raspberries and grapefruit taste together; often I smear a little spoonful of raspberry preserves on top of a sectioned grapefruit half for breakfast. When good fresh raspberries are abundant and melons are at their prime, I like this chilled compote for a simple summer dessert. Some of the raspberries are made into a quick sauce which—combined with the grapefruit juice—makes a fragrant, refreshing liquid. The rest are added to the compote at the last minute. Try to give this an hour in the refrigerator before serving, and chill your dessert bowls while you wait.

> 1 pint fresh raspberries
> 2 tablespoons confectioners' sugar
> 2 large ruby red grapefruit, halved and sectioned
> 1 tablespoon fresh lemon juice
> $^1/_2$ ripe cantaloupe
> ground nutmeg

Puree half the raspberries and the sugar in a food processor for about 20 seconds. Scrape down the sides and continue to puree for a few more seconds. If you don't mind the seeds, pour the puree into a bowl; otherwise strain it through a sieve into a bowl. Squeeze the grapefruit sections and their juice into the bowl with the raspberry puree. Stir in the lemon juice.

Cut the melon into bite-size chunks or balls and stir them into the compote. Chill the compote for an hour.

Divide the mixture evenly between dessert bowls, gently stirring some of the remaining fresh raspberries into each portion. Dust with nutmeg and serve.

# The Simple Garnish

Like the small but well-timed compliment to a friend, a seemingly insignificant dessert garnish can have a powerfully uplifting effect. It can add visual drama, excitement, a splash of color, a little texture to the landscape. And it can be a subtle reminder to those we're feeding just how very special they are to us.

There are a lot of little, easy ways we can dress up desserts with everything from fresh herbs to whipped cream. There are no hard rules, but some guiding principles are useful. Rule Number One is that enough is plenty. Less is generally more. Gobs of whipped cream can drown and upstage even the best pie or tart. A few threads of fresh mint add interest to many summer fruit desserts; a handful would have all the fascination of a compost heap. So go easy, whatever garnish you choose.

Fresh herbs and flowers are some of my favorite garnishes, because they're such a natural counterpart to a whole season of fine desserts. Strawberry shortcake is special on its own, but tuck a couple of fresh mint leaves into the whipped cream and you've added a flourish. A bowl of sliced

peaches and cold cream is lovely; throw on a few leaves of lemon thyme and it's celestial. Slivered rose petals add fragrant expectation to fruits, custards, and many creamy desserts. (But use only roses that haven't been sprayed with anything potentially harmful.)

Other edible plant garnishes include violets and some herb flowers, though use them sparingly when you're experimenting since many have peppery overtones. The scented basils make especially nice garnishes; try them with fruit and fruit-based sorbets and ices. Treat all leaves with care because they bruise easily. Cut them into thin slivers with scissors or a sharp knife.

Don't overlook a simple dusting of spice to accent your desserts. Ground nutmeg is a classic with cream and fruit; cardamom goes with blueberries (page 161); ground pepper with melon; ground cinnamon with sliced bananas, creamy chocolate desserts, and apple-based desserts, of course.

When a garnish adds contrasting texture as well, it fulfills a dual mission. Crumbled cookies over a dish of ice cream is as homey as you can get. Same for chopped, toasted nuts, and Pecan Praline (page 174).

I consider spirits a garnish as well. A splash of brandy over ice cream; some kirsch with your cherries or strawberries; or Kahlúa on Coffee Gelato (page 187) are adult touches many of us enjoy.

It often takes just a few seconds to add the right dessert garnish. Don't force it, but be prepared to seize the opportunity when it comes along.

# Shades of Red Sparkling
# Champagne Compote

*Makes 4 to 6 servings*

This is easily multiplied for a crowd, and it's a real crowd pleaser. It looks gorgeous too—chilled glasses of red summer fruit, with sparkling pink champagne poured over it. Choose your fruit carefully; it should be sweet enough to balance the relative dryness of the champagne. Currants are wonderful here, but they're hard to find, so just leave them out if they're unavailable. Adding a couple of drops of rose water to each serving contributes a tantalizingly sweet summer aroma to this sophisticated dessert.

1 pint fresh raspberries
1 cup pitted whole sweet cherries
1 pint strawberries
$1/_3$ cup red currants (optional)
1 bottle pink champagne, very cold
rose water

About 30 minutes before serving this, put wineglasses or glass dessert bowls in the freezer. When you're ready to serve, divide the fruit evenly between the glasses; if the strawberries are large, cut them into bite-size pieces.

Pour enough champagne into each glass to cover the fruit. Stir a couple of drops of rose water into one serving and taste; it should be evident, but not overpowering. Add more if necessary, then add the rose water to the other portions. Serve at once.

# Peach, Blueberry, and Basil Compote

*Makes 6 servings*

In this favorite summer compote, peaches are stewed in Beaujolais wine, and blueberries are added for the last couple of minutes. They gradually soften as the compote steeps overnight, releasing their juice and tinting the peaches a pretty shade of coral blue. A lovely, simple, and refreshing dessert for high summer.

1 cup Beaujolais
$^3/_4$ cup water
$^1/_2$ cup sugar
1 cinnamon stick
5 large ripe peaches, peeled and thickly sliced
1 cup blueberries
8 to 10 large basil leaves, plus a few extra for garnish

In a large nonreactive saucepan, bring the wine, water, sugar, and cinnamon stick to a near boil, stirring occasionally. Add the sliced peaches and simmer for 7 minutes, then stir in the blueberries. Simmer for another minute, then remove from the heat. Pour the mixture into a large pottery bowl and stir in the basil leaves.

Cool the compote to room temperature, then cover and refrigerate overnight. Serve in chilled dessert bowls, garnished with shredded basil leaves.

## Prunes Stewed in Port

*Makes 6 servings*

I seldom if ever eat plain dried prunes, but stewed prunes—soft, sweet, and suffused with the dark amber port syrup in which they've been poached—are quite another thing. In fact, I'll often make up a batch and keep them tightly covered in the fridge for a week or so at a time, serving myself a mini-portion several times a day, with light cream if I'm feeling so moved. Stewed prunes are great with coffee, for dessert; the flavors blend superbly. And they're just right with pound cake or a plain cookie, like the Whole Wheat Walnut Refrigerator Cookies (page 7).

1 pound pitted prunes
2 cups ruby port
1$^1/_2$ cups water
$^1/_3$ cup sugar
a 2-inch piece of vanilla bean, halved lengthwise
a long strip of lemon zest

Combine all of the ingredients in a large, nonreactive saucepan. Bring to a boil, stirring several times, then lower the heat and cover partially. Simmer the prunes gently for 25 to 30 minutes, until they are soft and tender. Remove from the heat, cover, and set aside to cool.

Discard the lemon zest and vanilla bean pieces. Transfer the prunes and their liquid to a large jar, cover, and refrigerate. Serve cold or at room temperature.

# Strawberries and Figs in Maple Balsamic Syrup

*Makes 4 servings*

Maple syrup and balsamic vinegar make a heavenly juice for dousing dried figs and fresh ripe strawberries. If you have the time, soak the figs in the liquid for an hour ahead of serving, basting the figs occasionally; otherwise, just toss the fruit in the juice and serve. If you can find a good fresh pineapple, add a handful of peeled chunks to the compote, soaking them in the liquid along with the figs. Serve with a nutty or shortbread cookie.

10 or 12 moist dried figs, preferably Black Mission; don't
  choose anything with a tough skin
4$^1/_2$ tablespoons pure maple syrup
1$^1/_2$ tablespoons balsamic vinegar
$^1/_4$ teaspoon vanilla extract
1 pint ripe strawberries
a little crushed fennel seed (optional)

Cut the stems off the figs, then cut the figs in half (if they're on the small side) or quarters. Put them in a small bowl so they fit snugly.

In a separate bowl, blend the maple syrup, vinegar, and vanilla and pour over the figs. Set aside for at least 10 minutes, basting the figs every few minutes.

Just before you are ready to serve, slice the strawberries into a bowl. Add the figs and toss the fruit gently so everything is coated. Serve the compote in little dishes, spooning some of the juice over each portion. Sprinkle with a few crushed fennel seeds (crushed with a rolling pin), if you like, and serve.

# Grapefruit and Raspberries in
# Red Wine Syrup

*Makes 4 to 6 servings*

This is a pleasing summer compote, served chilled—perhaps with a shortbread cookie or a scoop of Grapefruit Rosewater Sorbet (page 186). If you grow lemon thyme, scatter a few leaves over each serving.

$^3/_4$ cup red wine
$^1/_4$ cup sugar
1 cinnamon stick
1 or 2 long narrow strips of lemon zest
3 large grapefruits, preferably ruby red
2 tablespoons raspberry preserves
1 pint raspberries

In a small nonreactive saucepan, bring the wine and sugar to a boil. Add the cinnamon stick and lemon zest. Reduce the heat and simmer for 10 minutes. Remove from the heat.

Using a sharp knife, cut $^1/_4$ to $^1/_2$ inch of peel off each end of a grapefruit, deep enough to expose the flesh. Resting the grapefruit on one of the cut ends, trim all of the peel away from the flesh. With a sharp serrated knife, cut out the sections by running your knife down either side of the membranes; let the full sections fall into a large mixing bowl. After you've cut out the sections, squeeze the membrane shell over the bowl to get out all the juice. Repeat for the other grapefruits.

Remove the cinnamon stick and lemon zest from the wine syrup. Whisk the raspberry preserves into the syrup, then pour the syrup over the grapefruit. Stir. Cover and refrigerate for at least 2 hours.

Serve the compote in chilled dessert bowls, with a handful of fresh raspberries scattered over each serving.

# Citrus and Blueberry Compote with Orange-Flower Water

Colorful and fragrant, this compote makes a nice light ending to any summer meal. And it's sensational with shavings of the grapefruit sorbet (page 186) scattered over the top. If you have unsprayed rose petals in your yard, garnish the dessert top with a few thin slivers.

2 large grapefruit
2 large navel oranges
1½ cups fresh blueberries
1 tablespoon orange-flower water
3 tablespoons mild honey, like clover or orange blossom

Using a serrated knife, trim the ends of the grapefruits down to the flesh. Stand the grapefruit on a flat end and cut off all of the skin. Do the same for the oranges.

Holding the fruit over a bowl, cut out the sections, guiding your knife down through the flesh just to either side of each membrane. Let the sections fall into the bowl. As you finish each piece of fruit, squeeze the juice from the membrane skeleton over the fruit. Stir the blueberries and orange-flower water in with the other fruit.

Warm the honey in a small skillet, to thin it, then pour it into the compote and stir to blend. Cover and refrigerate if not serving right away. This is best eaten the same day.

# Chunky Summer Fruit Salsa

*Makes about 3 cups*

Sometimes we want a little more from fresh fruit than what it offers on its own; that's why I make this fresh fruit salsa. Perhaps the term "salsa" is a bit of a stretch for something so chunky, but the blend of sweet, tart, and fresh fruit flavors combined with mint really wakes up the taste buds the way a good fresh salsa does. I serve this with mascarpone crepes, over vanilla ice cream, with pound cake, and on its very own.

1 pound ripe plums, quartered, pitted, and cut in small
   chunks (about 2 cups)
1 cup fresh blueberries
$^{1}/_{4}$ cup pitted sour cherry halves (optional)
$2^{1}/_{2}$ tablespoons sugar
2 tablespoons fresh lime juice
1 tablespoon fresh lemon juice
1 to 2 tablespoons balsamic vinegar (optional)
5 or 6 fresh mint leaves, chopped

Just toss everything together in a big bowl, using the lesser amount of vinegar. Taste, and use more vinegar if you like. Cover and refrigerate for at least several hours before serving.

# Oranges and Pineapple in
# Maple Rum Sauce

*Makes 4 servings*

The older I get, the more I really appreciate quick fruit desserts such as this one; easy, refreshing, satisfying, and light. Here we cover cold orange slices and pineapple chunks with a maple rum sauce that's ready in less than 3 minutes. If good ripe pineapple is not available, substitute either grapefruit sections or canned pineapple chunks. This is great in summer or winter, with little scoops of vanilla ice cream.

4 navel oranges
1 cup pineapple chunks
2 tablespoons unsalted butter
$^{1}/_{3}$ cup maple syrup
2 tablespoons dark rum

Place 1 orange on a cutting board and cut a $^{1}/_{4}$-inch slice off the top and bottom. Using a sharp paring or fillet knife, slice the rind and white pith off the orange while you stand the orange on one of its cut ends. Lay the orange on its side and cut into $^{1}/_{4}$-inch-thick rounds.

As you cut each orange, lay overlapping slices in 4 dessert bowls with flat bottoms. Scatter about $1/4$ cup of pineapple chunks over the top of each. Cover and refrigerate until serving.

When you're ready to serve, melt the butter in a small saucepan. Add the maple syrup and bring to a rolling boil, stirring. Boil for 15 seconds then remove from the heat and whisk in the rum. Spoon a little of the sauce over each portion and serve right away.

# Blueberries and Melon in Blueberry Ginger Syrup

*Makes 4 to 5 servings*

Steeping blueberries in a ginger-infused simple syrup shades the liquid a pretty pinkish-blue. The cooled liquid is spooned over fresh melon and blueberries, then garnished with fresh mint. Look for the smaller wild blueberries; they have a slight but unmistakable sour tang that balances the sweetness of the syrup.

$1^1/2$ cups water
$1/2$ cup sugar
1 thumb-size piece of fresh ginger, unpeeled
2 thick lemon slices
$2^1/2$ cups blueberries
1 ripe cantaloupe, honeydew melon, or cranshaw melon
fresh mint leaves, thinly sliced, for garnish (optional)

In a small nonreactive saucepan, bring the water and sugar to a simmer. Cut the ginger into thin slices and add to the water with the lemon slices. Simmer for 8 minutes, then add $1/2$ cup of the blueberries and simmer for 2 more minutes. Pour the contents of the pan into a heatproof bowl and cool to room temperature. Strain the liquid and discard the solids. Cover the syrup and refrigerate until cold.

To serve, chill dessert bowls 30 minutes ahead. Put a handful of blueberries in each bowl, then cut the melon into bite-size chunks and add some to each. Ladle some of the syrup over each portion. Garnish with threads of fresh mint if you have it.

# Chilled Amaretto Plums with Almond Biscotti

*Makes 4 servings*

This is one of the easiest quick desserts I make with plums, an especially nice treatment if they're a little less than perfect, as plums tend to be in my part of the country. First I just toss the plum slices in sugar and let them sit for a few minutes to draw out the juices. Then I splash them with Amaretto and lemon juice. If you have some on hand, throw a piece or two of star anise into the bowl; it adds a wonderful perfume and delicate flavor. Plum skins can be bitter and chewy, so I like to peel the plums; a sharp serrated knife works better than a paring knife in this case. Serve a plateful of biscotti on the side, and don't be bashful about crumbling them right over the fruit.

> 6 ripe red plums
> 3 tablespoons sugar
> $1/3$ cup good-quality Amaretto
> juice of 1 lemon
> 1 or 2 pieces of star anise
> Almond Biscotti (page 13)

Peel the plums, then cut them in half. Slice the plums into a bowl then toss them with the sugar. Cover and set aside for 15 to 30 minutes.

Combine the remaining ingredients except the biscotti with the plums. Cover and refrigerate for at least 3 hours, or up to 12 hours before serving in chilled bowls with the biscotti on the side.

# Sour Cherries in
# Port Wine Syrup

*Makes 5 to 6 servings*

Brilliant red sour cherries take on an even deeper color and contrasting sweetness when they're macerated in port wine syrup. These are such a vibrant color that you should show them off in small glass dessert bowls or wineglasses. If you don't have a cherry pitter, unfold half of a paper clip and push the pit out with the point, inserting it opposite the stem end.

$2^{1}/_{2}$ to 3 cups pitted whole sour cherries
1 cup ruby port wine
$^{1}/_{2}$ cup sugar
2 thick orange slices

Put the pitted cherries in a ceramic bowl or soufflé dish that will accommodate them without a great deal of leftover space. Set them aside.

In a small nonreactive saucepan, bring the port, sugar, and orange slices to a boil. Reduce the heat and simmer for 10 minutes. Remove from the heat and cool for 5 minutes.

Pour the port syrup over the cherries and cool to room temperature. Cover and refrigerate until quite cold, preferably overnight or even longer. Discard the orange slices then serve the cherries in chilled glass bowls or glasses.

# Grape and Fig Compote
# with Bay Leaf

*Makes 6 servings*

I love the perfume of foods, and the way it adds to the expectation of the feast. Think what a farmstand full of ripe strawberries or lifting the lid on a favorite stew as it simmers does to your senses. Bay leaf has a sweet, spicy perfume, and in this Mediterranean-inspired compote—blended with honey, grapes, figs, and orange—it rises up to greet you with each spoonful. Market grapes are often disappointing where I live, but this treatment returns much of their promise. Serve this light dessert with biscotti, or spoon it on olive oil bread for an adventurous focaccia (page 101). This is best made several hours ahead if possible.

$^1/_2$ cup fresh-squeezed orange juice
$^1/_4$ cup mild honey, such as orange blossom or clover
2 or 3 small dried bay leaves
1 tablespoon balsamic vinegar
$2^1/_2$ cups seedless red or purple grape halves
8 to 10 dried figs (preferably Black Mission, but Turkish
   will do), sliced thin

In a small nonreactive saucepan, heat the orange juice, honey, bay leaves, and vinegar. Bring to a near-boil, then simmer for 5 minutes. Remove from the heat and cool for 1 hour.

Combine the grapes and figs in a bowl and pour the orange juice mixture over them. Stir, then cover and refrigerate for several hours, stirring the compote occasionally to coat everything with the liquid. Serve in small dessert dishes, and remember to remove the bay leaves first.

# Chilled Strawberry Melon Soup

*Makes 4 to 5 servings*

Even in the New Hampshire mountains we get some incredibly hot days, sometimes a whole string of them in the high 90s. When I can drag myself away from the lake long enough, I go fishing for this recipe and make up a batch of cold fruit soup. I'm not crazy about calling this a soup, since that's usually something savory and cooked, and this is neither. It's just a cold puree served in chilled bowls, with sliced strawberries floating on top. Ripe, juicy summer melon and strawberries are crucial. Though this is hardly any work at all, if you try to make this with inferior fruit it won't be worth even your modest effort.

strained juice of 1 orange
strained juice of 1 lime

$^1/_3$ cup sugar
1 ripe cantaloupe
1 pint ripe strawberries, cleaned and hulled
5 or 6 fresh basil leaves for garnish (optional)

Put the orange and lime juices into a glass measuring cup and add enough water to make 1 cup. Pour the liquid into a small nonreactive saucepan and add the sugar. Stir over low heat for a minute or two, just long enough to dissolve the sugar, then remove from the heat.

Halve the melons and clean out the seeds. Scoop the flesh into the bowl of a food processor. Add about 8 good-size strawberries and the reserved orange-lime juice and puree until smooth. (You may have to do this in 2 batches if your processor is small.) Strain the juice into a bowl, scraping and pushing on the solids to get out all the juice. Cover and refrigerate the juice.

About 30 minutes before you're ready to serve this, chill as many dessert bowls as you'll need. After 15 minutes, divide the "soup" evenly between them and put the bowls back in the freezer. Just before serving, slice the rest of the berries and add some slices to each bowl. If you're using it, cut the basil leaves into thin shreds and sprinkle some on top.

# Strawberry Wine Soup with Mint Cream

*Makes 4 servings*

This is as elegant as cold soups come; a red wine syrup, served with cold fresh berries, and topped with a mint-flavored cream and a garnish of fresh mint. For a cherry-berry variation on this, use very ripe, pitted whole sweet cherries instead of the strawberries in each bowl; but still use the strawberries to make the "broth."

$2^1/_4$ cups red wine (I like a Beaujolais here)
$^1/_3$ cup plus 2 tablespoons sugar
1 quart ripe strawberries
$^1/_2$ cup heavy cream
1 to 2 teaspoons white crème de menthe (see Note), *or* a
    *drop* of food-grade mint oil
fresh mint leaves for garnish

Put the red wine and $^1/_3$ cup of sugar in a small nonreactive saucepan. Bring to a boil, stirring occasionally, then boil until reduced by about half, about 7 to 10 minutes. Remove from the heat and pour it into a bowl to cool.

When the wine has cooled, pour it into a food processor. Hull about 8 or 10 good-size strawberries and add them to the wine. Process to a puree, then strain back into the original bowl. Chill the "broth" for at least 2 hours.

Chill your serving bowls about 30 minutes before you plan to serve this. Whip the cream to soft peaks, gradually adding the 2 tablespoons of sugar as it thickens. Beat in the crème de menthe to taste, up to 2 teaspoons, or add the mint oil.

To serve, hull the rest of the strawberries, slicing them in half if they're large. Add about $^1/_2$ cup of berries to each bowl, then divide the chilled "broth" between them. Top with a big spoonful of mint cream, and garnish with fresh mint.

*Note:* If you have both white and green crème de menthe on hand, you can use up to $^1/_2$ teaspoon of the green to add some mint color to the cream. Much more than that, however, tends to give it an unnatural-looking neon color.

# Poached Pear Halves in Ginger Syrup

*Makes 4 to 6 servings*

Part of me, the kid part I guess, has always been fond of canned pears. We used to have them a lot for dessert when I was a kid, which was entirely reasonable since there were 9 of us for dinner; even with just 4 kids, opening a can at the end of the day requires more energy than I can sometimes muster. Anyway, these are like canned, only better . . . softer, and more to my grown-up taste with a good ginger zing. All you do is poach ripe pears in a little pear juice, ginger, and sugar, then reduce the liquid to serve with them.

$1^1/_2$ cups pear juice, available at health food stores (see
  Note)
$^1/_4$ cup sugar
1 cinnamon stick (optional)
1 big thumb-size piece of fresh ginger
3 large ripe pears, peeled, halved, and cored

In a small nonreactive saucepan, bring the pear juice, sugar, and cinnamon stick, if you're using it, to a boil. As it heats, cut the ginger into quarter-size slivers and add them to the liquid along with the pear halves. Cook the pears at a lively simmer for about 20 minutes, until very tender; turn them occasionally with a spoon. Using a slotted spoon, transfer the pears to serving dishes.

Turn the heat up and boil the poaching liquid until only about $1/2$ cup of syrupy liquid remains. Strain, then spoon a little of the syrup into each bowl and serve as is.

*Note:* You can also use the thicker pear nectar, available at some supermarkets, thinned with water to a juicelike consistency.

# Sliced Sautéed Pears, Several Ways

*Makes 4 servings*

I love fresh ripe pears, but for dessert I usually want something a little more seductive; sautéed pears are just the thing. This treatment makes especially good sense if you have some less-than-perfect, or less-than-ripe pears, because the heat quickly renders the flesh soft, sweet, and juicy. It takes just a few minutes to slice the pears, and another 5 to sauté them. Beyond that you can serve them with chocolate sauce and vanilla ice cream, crumble molasses cookies over the top, or add a little cream to the pan at the last minute, serving them in this pan-caramel sauce. Each has its charms.

> 4 large ripe pears, preferably Bartletts; Boscs and Anjous
>   are also good
> 1 tablespoon unsalted butter
> 3 tablespoons packed light brown sugar
> 1 tablespoon fresh lemon juice

Peel, core, and slice the pears into slightly thicker than pie–size slices.

In a large nonreactive skillet, melt the butter. Add the sliced pears and sauté them over medium heat, stirring occasionally, for 3 minutes. Sprinkle on the brown sugar, increase the heat, and sauté for about 3 minutes more, until the slices are a light golden brown and tender. Stir in the lemon juice and cook for another few seconds.

Serve warm or at room temperature, alone or with one of the embellishments outlined on following page.

*Variations:* Serve with vanilla ice cream and 5-Minute Chocolate Sauce (page 198). Or crumble store-bought gingersnaps or Tess's Whole Wheat Ginger Cookies (page 17) over the top. Or add 1/2 cup heavy cream to the skillet about 45 seconds before the pears come off the heat. Bring to a boil and let the cream boil gently for 30 seconds. Serve the pears in their pan sauce.

# Grilled Peaches with Warm Blueberry Sauce

*Makes 4 servings*

Grilling fruit is a relatively new idea in dessert circles, but my guess is that in some form this practice has been going on since man's earliest encounter with fire. In any case, I'm a convert. Peaches are excellent grilled. They're juicy, yet firm enough to take the heat without falling apart. And they have a porous texture that soaks up the basting syrup nicely, in this case a reduction of port wine, honey, and a bay leaf. (Try this on plums and nectarines too.) While the peaches grill, I make this simple accompanying sauce with fresh blueberries and a bit of the port. If you like, a dab of peach ice cream on the side is perfect. Time this so the peaches go on the grill a few minutes after the coals are at their hottest.

1¼ cups ruby port wine
3 tablespoons honey
1 bay leaf
4 large just-ripe peaches
2 to 3 tablespoons olive oil
1 cup blueberries
1 tablespoon water

In a small nonreactive saucepan, bring the port, honey, and bay leaf to a boil. Boil the mixture for 3 minutes, then spoon off 2 tablespoons of the liquid and reserve. Continue to boil for another 8 to 12 minutes, until the liquid is reduced to about one-third of its original volume. Remove from the heat.

Peel and halve the peaches, removing the pits. Rub them on all surfaces with the olive oil and place them on the grill; the rack should be set 4 to 5 inches from the coals.

# Fruit Soups with Yogurt

All fruit soups are based on a "broth," a liquid medium such as a poaching liquid, wine, or fruit juice. But one of the simplest and most accessible broths is plain yogurt. This epiphany came to me during a summer visit to the Shaker Village in nearby Canterbury, where my friend, chef Jeffrey Paige, served a wonderful strawberry soup. Most chefs have a few super-simple recipes they fall back on when they're flat-out busy, and this was one of Jeff's. When I asked Jeff for the recipe, he didn't waste any words: "Just throw yogurt, strawberries, a little lemon juice, and sugar in the food processor. Don't forget the mint. You can't screw it up."

He's right; you can't. And since I don't have 50 people waiting in the wings for lunch, perhaps I can offer you this by way of general guidelines.

To serve up to 6 people, start by putting a handful of fresh mint leaves into a food processor with ½ cup sugar. Process well, breaking the mint into fine pieces. Add 1 quart of ripe strawberries and process to a puree. Now add a quart of plain yogurt—nonfat, lowfat, or regular—and process until smooth. Taste, adjusting the sweetening as desired, by adding up to $\frac{1}{3}$ cup honey.

Strawberries, of course, are only one option. You can use fresh raspberries or blackberries. However, since both have seeds, it is best to puree them alone first, then strain the puree. Blueberries are also excellent. I suggest cooking them first in a cupful of water and a tablespoon or two of sugar, to break down the skins. Puree and strain. In every case, the amount of sweetening and lemon juice you use is a matter of personal taste. Instead of lemon juice, try a bit of fruit vinegar instead.

The consistency of your fruit soups is also a personal matter, but I think they're most refreshing if they're not too thick. Plain water is the easiest way to adjust the consistency, but freshly squeezed orange juice adds a nice citrus tang. If you happen to have some poached fruit in the fridge, you can use some of the poaching liquid if it is compatible.

In any case, be sure to reserve enough of the fresh fruit—and mint leaves—to garnish your soup.

Grill the peaches, turning occasionally with tongs, for 6 minutes, then start basting them with the port syrup. Try not to be too sloppy with it, because drips may cause flare-ups. Continue to baste and grill for 6 more minutes. Move the peaches to the edge of the grill to keep them warm.

In a small nonreactive saucepan, combine the blueberries, reserved 2 tablespoons of port syrup, and the water. Bring to a boil, cover, and boil for 1 1/2 to 2 minutes, until the blueberries are soft. Remove from the heat.

Serve 2 peach halves to each person, with some of the sauce on the side.

# Grilled Bananas with Peanut Butter Whipped Mousse

*Makes 4 servings*

Here's something a little different, a little daring. Banana halves are rubbed with soft butter, gently grilled, then served with the same peanut butter and whipped cream combination I use with chocolate crepes. Speaking of which, if you can see the potential for a little warm chocolate sauce with this combination of bananas and peanut butter, go for it; try the 5-Minute Chocolate Sauce on page 198.

1 recipe Frozen Peanut Butter Mousse (page 94),
   refrigerated but not frozen
4 ripe but not overripe bananas
1 to 2 tablespoons unsalted butter, softened
warm chocolate sauce (optional)

As the peanut butter mousse chills, prepare the bananas: Leaving the skins on, cut them in half lengthwise and rub the flesh with the soft butter.

Place the banana halves on a rack over hot coals, flat side down; keep them toward the edges of the grill if the coals are very hot. Grill the bananas, without turning them, for about 8 to 10 minutes, until the flesh is soft.

Serve 2 halves per person, the ends touching, with a big spoonful of the peanut butter whipped mousse in the middle. Drizzle the chocolate sauce here and there if you're using it.

# Butterscotch Grilled Pineapple Slices

*Makes 6 servings*

Pineapple is the easiest of fruits to grill, sturdy as it is. I mean fresh pineapple, because canned is too fragile for this treatment. Here I cut thick slabs from a large ripe fruit, rub the pieces with oil, then begin coating them with a butterscotch basting sauce about halfway through. Go easy with the sauce at first, to minimize flare-ups; if they occur, move the slices to the side. Use more sauce as they finish cooking. At this point, don't be too concerned about an occasional flame because it will help to caramelize the surface, crème brûlée–style. You can even leave the skin on, which makes the slices easier to handle; just serve them with forks and sharp knives so folks can cut around the cores. These are great with ice cream or lightly sweetened sour cream.

1 large ripe pineapple
3 tablespoons light olive oil

## BUTTERSCOTCH BASTING SAUCE

$^1/_2$ cup packed light brown sugar
$^1/_2$ cup heavy cream
2 tablespoons unsalted butter
$^1/_4$ teaspoon vanilla extract

Using the center section of the pineapple, slice it into 6 round slabs, each about $^3/_4$ inch thick. Rub both sides with olive oil and lay them on the grill rack over coals slightly past their hottest stage. Grill the slices for about 8 minutes, turning them every couple of minutes.

While they grill, in a small saucepan, bring the brown sugar, cream, and butter to a boil. When it reaches a full boil, boil for 1 minute then remove from the heat. Stir in the vanilla extract.

After 8 minutes, begin basting the slices with the butterscotch sauce, turning often; baste and turn every minute or so for about 8 more minutes. If serious flare-ups occur, move the slices to safer ground near the perimeter of the grill.

Remove the slices to individual serving plates and spoon a little more of the sauce over the tops if there's any left.

# Chocolate and Coconut-Coated Pineapple

*Makes 4 servings*

Slices of pineapple are dipped in melted chocolate and rum and coated with toasted coconut. Then a small scoop of vanilla ice cream is plunked right in the center; it will look like you spent half the day putting this dessert together, but it takes scarcely 15 minutes. You can use canned pineapple, though the slices are a bit thin and fragile; better to select a ripe fresh pineapple and cut thick slices.

$1^1/_2$ cups flaked, sweetened coconut
3 tablespoons dark rum
1 tablespoon butter
3 ounces semisweet chocolate, coarsely chopped
4 rounds of pineapple, skin trimmed off, cut about $^3/_4$ inch
   thick
1 pint good-quality vanilla ice cream

Preheat the oven to 350°. Spread the coconut out on a baking sheet in a single layer. Toast for 10 to 15 minutes, stirring occasionally, until golden brown. Watch it carefully toward the end so it doesn't burn. Transfer to a large plate and cool.

Put the rum, butter, and chocolate in the top of a double boiler. Melt the chocolate over very hot water—5 to 10 minutes—then whisk to smooth. Remove the insert and place it at your work area. Cool the chocolate for 5 to 10 minutes.

Put the pineapple slices on paper toweling and blot them with another paper towel to remove the surface moisture. Line a small baking sheet with wax paper and make 4 circles of coconut on it, in a thin layer, slightly larger than the pineapple slices.

Dip both sides of each pineapple in the melted chocolate, then lay the individual slices on top of the coconut piles. Generously sprinkle the top of the pineapple with more toasted coconut. Cover and refrigerate for at least 15 minutes, or up to several hours.

Serve 1 slice of pineapple per person, with a small scoop of the vanilla ice cream right in the center.

# Maple Cinnamon Applesauce

*Makes about 2 cups*

I'm always reminded when I make applesauce just how simple it is, and how silly I am to buy the stuff at all. Here's a New England take on this old favorite, sweetened modestly with pure maple syrup and spiced with cinnamon; even when we buy plain applesauce, this is how we spiff it up. If you want to take this a step beyond basic, consider topping each serving with sautéed apple or pear slices, poached cranberries, or a dab of plain yogurt. More adult options include a spoonful of brandied fruit (page 166) or Cider Whiskey Sauce (page 206) on top.

4 large apples, peeled, cored, and roughly chopped
1 cup water
pinch of salt
$^1/_4$ cup maple syrup
juice of $^1/_2$ lemon
$^1/_4$ to $^1/_2$ teaspoon ground cinnamon

Put the apples, water, salt, and maple syrup in a medium-size nonreactive saucepan. Bring the water to a boil, cover, then reduce the heat to a low boil. Cook the apples for 15 minutes, tightly covered, until the apples are tender; check after 10 minutes to make sure there's enough water in the pot to keep the apples from sticking. When the apples are tender, remove them from the heat and cool for 15 minutes.

Transfer the apples to the bowl of a food processor and puree with the lemon juice and cinnamon, to taste. Keep it on the chunky or smooth side, whichever you prefer. Transfer to a bowl and cool. Refrigerate if not using right away.

# Gratin of Peaches and Raspberries

This is the easiest fruit gratin I know, and certainly one of my favorites. It has three elements: fresh fruit, a layer of White Chocolate Sour Cream Ganache (or just sour cream and sugar; see cheater's version below), and caramelized brown sugar. Though any fresh summer berry will do nicely, I like this combination of peaches and raspberries best, with its delightful contrast of textures. If you have a propane torch to caramelize the brown sugar, this is a real snap (see page 80). Otherwise, you'll have to run them under the broiler.

> 2 medium-size ripe peaches, peeled and thinly sliced
> $^1/_2$ pint raspberries
> 1 recipe White Chocolate Sour Cream Ganache (page 205), cold
> 4 to 6 tablespoons packed light brown sugar

Arrange one thick layer of peach slices and raspberries in the bottom of individual gratin dishes. If you don't have a propane torch, preheat the broiler and set the rack about 6 inches below the flame.

Smear a layer (about 2 tablespoons, give or take, depending on the size of the dishes) of the ganache over the fruit, spreading it evenly with a spoon.

Spread 1 to $1^1/_2$ tablespoons of brown sugar loosely over each serving. If you have a torch, sweep the flame back and forth over the brown sugar until it turns dark brown and bubbly. This will take only a matter of seconds. If you're using the broiler, put the dishes in a shallow casserole. Surround the dishes with a tray's worth of ice, then add enough cold water to come two-thirds up the sides of the dishes. Run the casserole under the broiler and leave it there for 1 to 2 minutes, until the brown sugar is dark brown and bubbly. Remove the dishes from the ice water with a spatula and serve.

*Variation:* If you'd rather not make the White Chocolate Sour Cream Ganache, here's an easier way: Mix 1 cup cold sour cream with confectioners' sugar to taste. Don't make it too sweet; you want to taste a slight tang. Use this sweetened sour cream in place of the ganache and proceed as above.

# Blueberries with
# Sweet Cheese and Cardamom

*Makes 4 to 6 servings*

Somewhere along the way—probably because I've used it with everything under the sun—I learned how wonderful cardamom tastes with blueberries. (Try it sometime in your blueberry pies.) Here I use ground cardamom as a garnish over sweetened cream cheese, which I spoon over the berries; just a pinch is all you need. The sweet cheese will remind you of the cream cheese icing you put on carrot cake; if you're an unreformed icing-bowl licker, this dessert essentially legitimizes your addiction. At the end of August, when blueberry and blackberry seasons overlap, try both berries together here.

1 pint blueberries
2 tablespoons sugar
juice of ¹/₂ lemon

SWEET CHEESE

8 ounces cream cheese, softened
¹/₃ cup sugar
¹/₄ teaspoon vanilla extract
1 teaspoon fresh lemon juice
milk (optional)
ground cardamom for garnish

In a bowl, mix the berries, sugar, and lemon juice, then divide the fruit evenly between your dessert bowls.

Using an electric mixer, beat the cream cheese, sugar, vanilla, and lemon juice until smooth and soft; it should be of thickish, pouring consistency. If it seems too thick for you, thin with a spoonful or two of milk.

Spoon the cheese over the fruit and garnish each serving with a big pinch of ground cardamom.

*Note:* If you have really excellent fruit, and you'd rather not sugar the berries, just put them right in your bowl as is and spoon the cheese over the top.

# Pecans, Creamed Blue Cheese, and Sliced Fall Fruit

*Makes 4 to 6 servings*

This dessert plate was inspired by a salad Karen and I enjoy at a restaurant in Hanover, New Hampshire. The salad is garnished with crumbled blue cheese and a half dozen or so sugared pecans. And it works quite well, the sharpness of the cheese offsetting the sweetness of the pecans. I've done essentially the same thing here, using praline pecans. Too much candy would ruin the effect, so after the praline has cooled I break the nuts away from the surrounding hardened sugar. Then I arrange the pecans on a platter, with sliced apples and pears and a small mound of cream cheese mixed with blue cheese.

1 recipe Pecan Praline (page 174), modified as below
1/3 cup crumbled blue cheese
one 3-ounce package cream cheese
2 large apples
2 large ripe pears
juice of 1 lemon

Make the praline as directed, with these changes: Working very quickly, drop the nuts into the saucepan and stir to coat. Quickly lift them out with a slotted spoon, transferring them to a buttered baking sheet. Spread the pecans out in a single layer with a fork. Cool thoroughly.

Break as much hardened sugar away from the pecans as possible, and put the pecans on a serving platter.

Using a fork, in a small bowl, mix the cheeses; leave the mixture a little chunky and uneven. Scrape the cheese into a pile on the platter.

Peel, core, and slice the fruit thickly. Toss in a bowl with the lemon juice, then arrange the fruit on the platter too. Serve with little plates and forks; everyone will figure out what to do.

# Grapes, Feta Cheese, and Basil

*Makes 6 to 8 servings*

I love this little sweet and savory bite for a light summer dessert. You choose perfect basil leaves, spread or pipe creamy feta cheese on them, and top with a grape; in one bite you get 3 distinct and clear flavors. Since this takes just minutes to prepare, wait until you're ready so the basil doesn't get tired just sitting around on the dessert tray. I suggest piping the cheese mixture onto the leaves, if that appeals to you, but the fact is I'm not and never have been much of a piper myself; I just neatly spoon it on.

24 (approximately) clean fresh basil leaves, each about $1^1/_2$
   to 2 inches long
$^1/_2$ cup crumbled feta cheese
sour cream
$^1/_4$ pound seedless green grapes

If possible, select basil leaves with a natural concavity; this gives you a handy place to put the cheese. Chill a pretty dessert plate to put these on.

Using a fork, mix the feta cheese with just enough sour cream to make it creamy enough to hold together; start with a tablespoon and increase it from there as necessary.

Spoon or pipe about a teaspoon of the cheese onto each leaf. Press a whole grape into the cheese, just enough to secure it; if the grapes look too big, cut them in half lengthwise and place them in the cheese, flat side down. Arrange them on the chilled plate and serve.

# Creamy Stuffed Peaches with Raspberry Sauce

*Makes 4 to 6 servings*

Here are a couple of ways to stuff small ripe summer peaches: with a creamy blend of mascarpone and marmalade, or with a scoop of your favorite ice cream; I'd choose vanilla, butter pecan, or perhaps even a fruit sorbet. These aren't so much stuffed as they are reassembled, the halves sandwiching the ice cream or mascarpone. It isn't absolutely necessary, but depending on whom you're serving, you may want to peel the peaches as described below; it's a thoughtful gesture if you're having guests. But you can skip that step if you don't mind the skins. The raspberry sauce is perfect with this.

$^2/_3$ cup cold mascarpone cheese
$^1/_4$ cup orange marmalade
4 to 6 small, just-ripe peaches (1 per person)
1 recipe Raspberry Sauce (page 200)
1 pint superpremium ice cream (if you aren't using the mascarpone filling)

If you're using the mascarpone filling, in a small bowl, combine the mascarpone and marmalade. Fold together several times, leaving the mixture streaky, then cover and place in the freezer for an hour.

Bring a large saucepan of water to a boil. Once it begins to boil, add half the peaches you'll be using. Boil the peaches for 30 to 45 seconds, then transfer them to a plate with a slotted spoon. As soon as they've cooled enough to handle, score the peaches down to the pit with a sharp knife, along their natural crevice. Turn the halves in opposite directions, to twist them apart. Slide the peels off, then carefully remove the pit. Repeat for the remaining peaches, and let them all cool.

When you're ready to assemble them, slice about $^1/_2$ inch off the top of all the peach halves, so they'll stand up straight on the plate. Scoop about 2 generous table-spoons of the mascarpone mixture on a peach half, and press another half on the other side, making a sort of peach sandwich. Keep the flat edges on the same end. Place the stuffed peach on a plate, flat side down, and spoon raspberry sauce around the bottom of the peach. Repeat for the remaining peaches. If you're using ice cream, put a small scoop between the peach halves and proceed as above.

# Strawberry Blossoms

*Makes 4 servings*

Here's a springtime dessert that's as lovely to look at as it is to eat—delicate phyllo cups, filled with strawberry whipped cream and topped with fresh sliced strawberries. This is the sort of pretty dessert your mom would love for Mother's Day, or even something you could make for a small dinner party since the phyllo cups can be made a day or two in advance; the rest of the assembly takes only a few minutes. I've given one suggestion for an instant sauce you can drizzle over the tops, but it's optional if you want to keep things as simple as possible.

1 quart ripe strawberries
$^1/_3$ cup granulated sugar
1 cup whipping cream
4 Sweet Phyllo Baskets (page 108)
confectioners' sugar to dust on top
3 tablespoons red currant jelly (optional)

Slice 2 cups of the strawberries into a bowl and sprinkle them with about half the granulated sugar. Set aside for 5 minutes. Put them in a food processor and process for just a few seconds, to make a *coarse* puree; be careful not to liquefy them. Pour them into a sieve set over a bowl and let them drain.

Whip the cream until it holds soft peaks. Add the rest of the sugar and continue to beat until the cream is stiff but not curdled. Gently push any excess liquid out of the processed berries, then fold the berries into the whipped cream. Reserve the berry juice.

Slice a few of the remaining berries and place them in the phyllo cups. Mound plenty of the strawberry cream in each cup, then top with more sliced berries. Scatter extra sliced berries on each plate around the cups.

Dust the tops of the cups with confectioners' sugar and serve, with or without the following sauce: Pour the strawberry juice into a small nonreactive saucepan. Stir in the red currant jelly and bring to a boil. When the jelly melts, and the liquid turns syrupy and a little thick—a minute or so—remove from the heat. Drizzle a little sauce over the center of each serving.

# Strawberries Romanoff

*Makes 6 servings*

Do you like to play with your ice cream until it gets all smooth and creamy? Then you'll love this! It's only fair that something so good and simple never goes out of style. Be sure to chill your serving dishes beforehand, and plan to serve this right away.

1 quart fresh strawberries, sliced
$1/3$ cup confectioners' sugar
1 cup good and cold heavy cream
1 pint good-quality vanilla ice cream, slightly softened
Grand Marnier or Cointreau (optional)

Chill your serving dishes and the bowl you'll whip the cream in. Slice the strawberries into a bowl and sprinkle with about half of the sugar. Set aside.

Whip the cream in the chilled bowl until it holds soft peaks. Add the rest of the sugar and beat for a few more seconds.

Put the ice cream in a third bowl and work it with a wooden spoon until it's pliable, but not too soft. Fold the whipped cream into the ice cream.

Immediately spoon the creamed mixture into your chilled bowls. Top each portion with a big spoonful of strawberries and their juice. If you like, sprinkle a little Grand Marnier or Cointreau over the top. Serve at once.

# Dried Fruit in Brandy

Here is an indispensable little item in the simple dessert maker's bag of tricks. The quantities are necessarily vague, since this can be made in any amount you might like. I make up little jars of brandied dried fruit in early fall, for holiday gift giving, and I keep a big bottle on hand that lasts for months. Though most any dried fruit can be soaked this way, I prefer some combination of raisins, pears, cranberries, and cherries, generally fewer of the latter two because they're most expensive.

What can you do with these fruits? I love to spoon a little over vanilla ice cream, pound cake, or just a puddle of Crème Anglaise (page 199). They're wonderful with Chocolate Pâte (page 91), or baked apples. A couple of heaping tablespoons add interest to apple or pear pie filling. I could go on and on. Start by finding suitable jars; for gift giving, the French preserve jars with hinged lids and rubber gaskets are very nice. Then you can gauge approximately how much fruit you will need.

> dried fruit: some combination of pears, raisins, cranberries, cherries; prunes and raisins are also good together
> 1 vanilla bean
> Grand Marnier or Cointreau
> 1 bottle of brandy

Clean and rinse the jars well with very hot water. Dry well. Put alternating layers of fruit in the jars (rather than putting all of one kind of fruit together on the top or bottom). Or you can use separate jars for each fruit.

Slit the vanilla bean in half lengthwise. Put a long piece of it inside each jar. Pour about ¹/₄ cup of Grand Marnier or Cointreau over the fruit—about half that much for small jars—then add enough brandy to cover the fruit. Invert the jars several times to mix the spirits.

Store the jars in a cool cupboard for at least 1 month before using, occasionally inverting the jars to move the liquid. If the brandy level drops in the first week, add enough to cover the fruit. Spoon out the brandy and fruit as needed.

# *Hazelnut-Crusted Figs with Honey Yogurt Sauce*

*Makes 4 servings*

I've often bemoaned that fresh figs in New Hampshire are about as rare as springtime without mud in these parts. Lacking the fresh item, I'm a big fan of dried figs, which I like to eat plain for dessert, poached in wine, or tossed into a favorite pear pie. Here's another way to enjoy them simply, bathed in warm honey then coated with toasted chopped hazelnuts. They're really divine this way and the tangy orange-scented yogurt sauce provides the perfect balance to the crunchy-sweet figs. These can be made ahead and refrigerated for an hour or so, but the less chilling the better so the hazelnuts retain their crunch. If the figs are cold, let them sit at room temperature for 20 minutes before serving.

1 cup toasted hazelnuts (page 20)
12 to 16 medium-size dried figs, either Black Mission or
  Turkish (I prefer the former)
$^1/_2$ cup mild honey, such as orange blossom or clover
1 cup cold plain yogurt
finely grated zest of 1 orange
fresh pear slices (see Note)

Finely chop the toasted hazelnuts by hand and transfer to a plate. Set aside.

Snip the stems off the figs and cut them in half or quarters, lengthwise, whichever seems more bite-size.

In a small saucepan, heat the honey, stirring. When it is hot, turn off the heat and add 6 or 7 fig sections to the pan; don't crowd them. Spoon a little honey over each one, to coat, then transfer the figs to the hazelnut plate with a slotted spoon. Roll the figs in the hazelnuts, coating them well. Transfer the figs to another plate and set them aside.

Put the yogurt in a small bowl and whisk in just enough of the honey from the pan to sweeten it slightly, to taste. Stir in the orange zest. Cover and refrigerate until ready to serve.

Put several figs and pear slices on each serving plate and pass the sauce separately.

*Note:* If raspberries happen to be in season, a pile of them on the side of each plate—instead of the pears—is a wonderful idea.

# Medjool Dates with Orange Almond Paste

*Makes 6 servings*

I borrowed this idea from one of my favorite cooks, Deborah Madison, who wrote the wonderful *Greens Cookbook* (Bantam, 1987) and *The Savory Way* (Bantam, 1990). Ms. Madison makes these with real homemade almond paste, but mine is a shortcut version made with toasted and ground unblanched almonds. The nuts are bound with a little orange juice and a bit of honey, then packed on top of date halves. (The nut mixture can be made several days ahead and refrigerated.) They're a delicious little afterdinner tidbit, served alone or on a plate with orange wedges, grapes, and melon slices.

1 cup toasted whole unblanched almonds, cooled (page 20;
   see Note)
$1/4$ cup packed light brown sugar
2 tablespoons fresh orange juice
1 tablespoon honey
9 big, soft Medjool dates

Combine the cooled nuts in a food processor with the brown sugar. Process until the nuts are finely ground. In a cup, mix the orange juice and honey and gradually pour them into the ground nuts with the machine running. Stop the machine when the mixture clumps up, about 5 seconds.

Neatly slit the dates in half lengthwise. Remove the pits and pack each half with a little of the ground nut mixture, mounding it slightly. Arrange on a plate and cover until serving.

*Note:* I like the flavor of roasted almonds, with the skins on. However, for a more delicate almond flavor you can use blanched almonds and not bother to toast them.

# Ice Cream, Sorbet, and Other Frozen Desserts

Time was—and not all that long ago—that making frozen desserts at home meant only one thing: the Big Old-Fashioned Ice Cream Maker. In its day, this contraption was lots of fun, a gastronomic icon of American largesse. You'd drag it up from the cellar every Fourth of July, dust it off, and fill the metal canister with tons of fresh strawberries and oceans of cream. Then you'd pack it into the wooden bucket with ice and rock salt ("Who took the rock salt from the tool shed?"; "Hey, we need more ice!") and all the kids would take a turn cranking. When they lost interest, you could always count on Uncle Bob to finish the grunt work. Then everyone would fight over who got to lick the dasher. At the end of the weekend, you'd clean it up, and stick it back in the cellar until next summer.

Today, Uncle Bob's cranking arm isn't what it used to be, and neither are frozen desserts. Not that we've outgrown good old-fashioned ice cream. Not on your life! And some of us still prefer the old-style freezers. But we've expanded our horizons, acquired new tastes. And this chapter on frozen desserts reflects those changes.

I think the advent of the sealed-in coolant ice cream freezers—pioneered by Donvier—did a lot to revitalize our interest in frozen desserts. These metal cylinders with a chemical coolant permanently sealed inside made it easy for the average family to make ice cream even when Uncle Bob wasn't around. The new generation of ice cream makers eliminates the mess and bother of all that ice and rock salt. And because they need only an occasional turn of the dasher, one person can put the finishing touches on the blackberry cobbler and make ice cream at the same time.

Whatever your choice of ice cream freezer, here you'll find plenty of ways to chill out. There are ice creams, of course, and I must warn you I'm not one to skimp on ingredients: good fruit; cream; and often egg yolks for richness, flavor, and body.

Though I'm no less fond of ice cream than I used to be, I've discovered that a homemade ice or sorbet leaves me feeling just as satisfied as ice cream does after a meal.

Most ices are based on a simple formula of sugar water and fruit puree, but the potential for variety is vast and exciting. And if it simplifies life somewhat, you don't even need an ice cream freezer to make them; they can all be still-frozen, using the technique I describe on page 182.

One relative newcomer to the American dessert scene is the Italian semifreddo, in texture somewhere between a frozen mousse and a soft ice cream. You'll find a couple of variations here, along with old-fashioned American-style favorites like New England maple rum ice cream, and a celestial Peanut Cloud Pie.

# French Vanilla Bean Ice Cream

*Makes about 1 quart*

This is right at the top of the richness scale of frozen desserts, and meant to be taken in small doses; a single batch, with a quart of fresh sliced strawberries, could easily serve 8 people for dessert. I make this only when I can find fresh plump vanilla beans at my local health food store. Fresh vanilla beans are soft and fragrant, rather than dry and skinny. I'm not a fetishist about vanilla beans; I simply prefer, on occasion, the intoxicatingly fresh flavor and perfume of vanilla beans over vanilla extract, with the flecks of vanilla bean in the ice cream providing added texture. Because the flavor of fresh vanilla is so wonderful on its own, don't serve this with chocolate sauce or anything else that would compete too much.

> 2 cups light cream
> $^3/_4$ cup plus 2 tablespoons sugar
> 1 plump vanilla bean
> 4 egg yolks
> $1^1/_2$ cups heavy cream

In a medium-size nonreactive saucepan, combine the cream and sugar. Cut the vanilla bean in half at its waist, then halve it lengthwise. Using the edge of a paring knife, scrape the seeds out of the bean into the cream; you'll never get them all, but do a reasonable job. Drop the sections of the bean into the cream.

Heat the cream, stirring, until the surface shimmers and the sugar melts, 3 to 4 minutes. Remove from the heat, cover, and let steep for 30 minutes. Remove the pieces of the bean with a slotted spoon and discard them.

In a mixing bowl, whisk the egg yolks. Gradually stir in the warm cream, then pour the mixture back into the saucepan. Cook over medium-low heat, stirring constantly, for about 10 minutes, until it reads 180° on a thermometer. Pour the mixture into a bowl and cool to room temperature. Cover and chill for 2 to 3 hours, or overnight.

Blend the heavy cream with the chilled mixture and pour into the freezer of an ice cream maker. Freeze according to the manufacturer's directions.

# Maple Rum Ice Cream with Pecan Praline

*Makes a little less than 1 quart*

You've *never* had a maple pecan ice cream like this one before. And chances are you'll never settle for less after you've tried it. Since there are no other competing major flavors, you need only ¹/₂ cup of maple syrup for the flavor to shine right through; the balance of the sweetening comes from the sugar. The praline is a good nutty topper, if you go for crunchies with your ice cream, but you can always skip it and use plain chopped pecans if you'd rather.

> 2 cups light cream
> ¹/₂ cup sugar
> 3 egg yolks
> ¹/₂ cup maple syrup
> 2 tablespoons dark rum
> ¹/₂ teaspoon vanilla extract
> 1 cup heavy cream
> Pecan Praline (optional—page 174)

In a heavy saucepan, heat the cream and sugar, stirring, until the sugar dissolves, about 3 to 4 minutes. Remove from the heat.

In a medium-size bowl, whisk the egg yolks. Stir in the hot cream a little at a time; begin with several tablespoons, eventually pouring it in in a slow, steady stream. Put the pan back on the heat and turn the heat to medium-low. Cook, stirring constantly, for about 10 minutes; when the mixture is done it will have thickened slightly and reached 180° on a candy thermometer.

# A Good Reason to Keep Ice on Hand

To fast-forward the time to great homemade ice cream, keep a big bag of ice on hand in the freezer.

Most ice cream or sorbet recipes, mine included, advise you to cool the warm liquid that makes your frozen dessert base. The standard way of doing this is to let it cool at room temperature, then move it to the fridge to chill.

But it's much quicker to fill a big bowl with ice and cold water, then place the bowl with your warm liquid right in it. Simply stir the mixture from time to time, and within about 15 minutes your liquid will be cold enough to proceed with the freezing process.

Pour the liquid into a bowl and stir in the maple syrup. Cool to room temperature. Cover and chill for several hours, or overnight.

Blend the rum, vanilla, and heavy cream into the chilled mixture. Pour into an ice cream freezer and freeze according to the manufacturer's directions.

Serve with the Pecan Praline sprinkled over the top of each portion.

# Pecan Praline

*Makes about 1 1/2 cups praline*

When you caramelize sugar and coat nuts with it, you end up with praline. Praline can be chopped coarsely, or ground to a finer consistency in the food processor, then used to dress up many desserts. I like it over poached pears, on top of ice cream (especially maple), folded into whipped cream—when you keep it around, you'll find many uses for it. You can make praline from other toasted nuts too; just follow the same procedure—try almonds or hazelnuts.

1/2 **cup water**
1 1/4 **cups sugar**
1 1/4 **cups toasted pecans, cooled (page 20)**

Lightly butter a large baking sheet and set it aside.

In a small or medium-size saucepan, combine the water and sugar. Gradually bring to a boil over medium heat, stirring once or twice as it begins to boil. Boil the syrup for 10 to 15 minutes, undisturbed, until the sugar turns a medium amber color; it may help to momentarily pull the pan off the heat so the bubbling subsides and you can better judge the color. When the sugar is done, you should notice a distinct caramelized sugar smell, and see puffs of smoke, as opposed to steam, coming from the pan.

Remove the pan from the heat and immediately stir in the cooled pecans. Stir with a wooden spoon, to coat all of the nuts, then scrape the mixture out onto the buttered sheet. Spread the nuts around in a mostly single layer, and let cool thoroughly.

When the praline is totally cooled, scrape it off the sheet. Chop coarsely by hand, or break the mixture into a food processor and grind to a fairly fine consistency. Store at room temperature in an airtight container. It will keep for weeks.

# Hardening Ice Cream and Ices

Most homemade ice cream and sorbet cannot freeze hard enough during stir-freezing (in your ice cream maker) to be served right from the cylinder, especially in hot weather. The ice cream tends to turn to soup before you have a chance to enjoy it.

That's where hardening comes in. Hardening means repacking your ice cream and placing it in your home freezer, so the ice cream has a chance to firm up. Hardening improves the texture, but it also gives the flavor elements of your frozen dessert time to blend and mellow.

To harden your frozen desserts chill a bowl, well ahead, large enough to hold the contents. Using a rubber spatula, scrape the ice cream into the bowl, pushing it down gently and quickly in the bowl to eliminate air pockets where ice crystals can form. Cover and freeze for an hour or two, until the ice cream has reached optimal semi-firm serving texture.

If you have a Donvier or other sealed-in coolant–type ice cream maker, *don't* harden the ice cream directly in the freezer cylinder even though it fits nicely in your home freezer. The freezing efficiency of that type of cylinder can be easily damaged if you scratch the cylinder walls with a serving spoon.

# Old-Fashioned Strawberry Ice Cream

*Makes about 1 quart*

Old-fashioned strawberry ice cream doesn't skimp on the basics, like sugar, eggs, and cream. It uses only the freshest, local, drop-dead-ripe berries. And it makes even the best superpremium brand seem pale by comparison. That's what this one is all about. For an unforgettable strawberry shortcake, substitute this ice cream for the traditional whipped cream.

1 cup heavy cream
1 cup light cream
1 cup sugar
2 egg yolks
2 cups sliced strawberries
1 teaspoon vanilla extract

In a medium-size nonreactive saucepan, combine the creams and $1/2$ cup of the sugar. Stir over moderate heat, until the sugar dissolves, 3 to 4 minutes. Remove from the heat.

Whisk the yolks in a small bowl, then whisk in several tablespoons of the hot cream. Do this several times, to temper the yolks, then pour the yolk mixture back into the cream. Turn the heat on medium-low and cook, stirring nonstop, for 8 to 10 minutes, until it reaches 180°; don't let it boil. Pour the cream into a shallow round casserole and cool to room temperature. Cover and chill thoroughly.

Meanwhile, in the bowl of a food processor, combine the strawberries with the remaining $1/2$ cup of sugar. Puree until not quite smooth; a few little chunks are good. Pour into a bowl, and stir in the vanilla. Cover and refrigerate.

After the cream has chilled, transfer it and the puree to an ice cream freezer and freeze according to the manufacturer's instructions.

# Lemon Ice Cream

*Makes about 1 quart*

My family and I love this with fresh sliced strawberries or peaches, with shortbread cookies on the side. Because this ice cream is made without eggs or coloring, it doesn't have the lemon color you may expect; it's a creamy white. But the taste of fresh lemon is unmistakable.

> 3 cups light cream
> 1$^1$/$_2$ cups sugar
> 1 cup heavy cream
> $^1$/$_2$ cup fresh lemon juice
> 1$^1$/$_2$ teaspoons lemon extract

In a small nonreactive saucepan, combine 1 cup of the cream with the sugar. Heat, stirring, until the sugar melts, about 3 to 4 minutes, then scrape the mixture into a bowl. Cool to room temperature, then chill for 2 hours in the refrigerator.

Blend the rest of the ingredients with the chilled liquid. Transfer the mixture to an ice cream freezer and freeze according to the manufacturer's instructions.

# Pumpkin Ice Cream

*Makes almost 1 quart*

Much as I love the fresh fruit summer ice creams, this might be my favorite ice cream of all. It's certainly one of the easiest since the predominant flavoring—pumpkin—comes right out of the can. If you want to turn this into a dressy dessert, serve it with thin slices of pound cake and 5-Minute Chocolate Sauce (page 198). Or with a nutty cookie, perhaps biscotti. A few chopped pecans and a little maple syrup drizzled over the top are great too.

> 1 cup light cream
> 1 cup packed light brown sugar

3 egg yolks
1 cup canned (cold pack) pumpkin
1 cup heavy cream
$^1/_2$ teaspoon vanilla extract
$^1/_2$ teaspoon *each* ground cinnamon, ground nutmeg, and
   ground cloves

In a medium-size nonreactive saucepan, combine the light cream and brown sugar. Cook over medium heat just until the sugar dissolves, 3 to 4 minutes, then remove from the heat.

In a medium-size bowl, whisk the egg yolks. Whisk about half of the hot liquid into the yolks, about $^1/_4$ cup at a time, then pour the tempered yolks back into the saucepan with the rest of the liquid. Cook the mixture over medium-low heat, stirring more or less nonstop, for about 8 minutes, until the temperature reaches 180° on a candy thermometer. Remove from the heat and transfer the mixture to a bowl. Cool to room temperature, then cover and refrigerate for at least 2 hours.

When you're ready to proceed, whisk the remaining ingredients into the chilled mixture. Transfer to the freezer of an ice cream maker and freeze according to the manufacturer's instructions.

# Toasted Almond Ice Cream Loaf
# with Fresh Cherries

*Makes 8 servings*

When I was a kid I used to *live* for the Good Humor ice cream man. Every evening after dinner I'd hear the little tinkle of his bell, then go dashing off into the house to collect change before I—and the rest of the neighborhood—flagged him down. Kids being creatures of habit, I always ordered a toasted almond. I don't run after Good Humor trucks anymore—haven't seen any in years—but I do occasionally make this molded ice cream dessert with my favorite childhood flavors. And it's no more complicated than a lazy summer evening, just layers of vanilla ice cream and ground toasted almonds and coconut; sliced cherries add a bright, fruity touch. Before you begin the recipe, transfer the ice cream to the fridge for 30 minutes so it will be easy to spread.

1 cup flaked, sweetened coconut

1 cup toasted whole almonds, cooled (page 20)

1 tablespoon sugar

$^1/_2$ gallon vanilla ice cream (I like Breyer's)

$^1/_4$ pound fresh sweet cherries, such as Bings, pitted and
halved (see Note)

Line a 6-cup loaf pan with a double layer of plastic wrap, leaving at least a 3-inch over-hang on the long edges. Place it in the freezer.

Preheat the oven to 325°. Spread the coconut on a large cookie sheet and toast for 8 to 10 minutes, until golden brown. Watch it carefully, because it can scorch easily. Dump the coconut onto a plate and cool thoroughly.

Put the coconut, almonds, and sugar into a food processor and grind to a crunchy meal; it shouldn't get too fine. Set half aside for immediate use; cover and refrigerate the rest.

To assemble the mold, sprinkle the bottom of the mold with some of the chopped mixture. Spread enough ice cream in the mold to come one-third of the way up; if the ice cream is still stiff, work it with the back of a big spoon to loosen it up. Sprinkle the first layer generously with the chopped mixture. Make 2 more layers of ice cream and chopped stuff, ending with the chopped stuff almost level with the top of the pan. Cover with foil and freeze for several hours, until hard, or overnight. Chill a serving plate for the mold.

When you're ready to serve, unmold the ice cream by pulling up on the plastic. Remove the plastic and put the mold on the chilled plate. Generously cover on all sides with the reserved crunchy mixture, gently patting it into the surfaces with your hands. Cut into thick slices and serve with the sliced cherries.

*Note:* If the cherries are less than perfect, sugar them lightly and sprinkle with lemon juice.

# Blueberry Lime Sorbet

*Makes almost 1 quart, 6 servings*

This is so good that Karen is totally out of control when there's some in the freezer—and she doesn't even *like* blueberries! I use a little trick here that builds a lot of flavor into sorbets: using some fruit juice concentrate for the sweetener. So long as you don't overdo it, the concentrate adds some pizazz to your sorbet without hiding the dominant flavors; here, for example, I use tangerine concentrate, and it blends beautifully with the blueberry and lime. Serve with any fresh summer berry, including the obvious, and wedges of lime.

$1^1/_3$ cups water
$^1/_2$ cup sugar
$^1/_2$ cup tangerine juice concentrate
$^1/_4$ cup fresh lime juice
1 cup blueberries

In a medium-size nonreactive saucepan, combine the water, sugar, and tangerine juice concentrate. Heat, stirring, until the sugar has dissolved, about 3 to 4 minutes.

Transfer the liquid to the bowl of a food processor and add the lime juice and blueberries. Process for 20 to 30 seconds, until the mixture is totally liquefied except for bits of blueberry skins. Strain through a wire sieve, pushing the juice out of the berry skins. Cool to room temperature, then cover and refrigerate until cold.

Transfer the cold liquid to an ice cream maker and freeze according to the manufacturer's instructions. Pack the sorbet in a chilled bowl and freeze until firm enough to serve.

# Raspberry Peach Sorbet

*Makes about 1 quart, 5 to 6 servings*

Perhaps the best testimonial I can offer for this peak-of-summer sorbet comes from my son Ben, who said—as if I had just told him he could buy the mountain bike of his dreams—"Wow! Is this refreshing!!" And so it is. One of my favorite ways to eat this is with chunks of chilled, almost-frozen watermelon; I put the pieces of watermelon in dessert bowls, cover, and stick them in the freezer for about 30 minutes. Then I spoon this right over the top. You could, if you have it on hand, drizzle on a bit of framboise. Or serve small scoops of this with vanilla ice cream, surrounded by raspberries and peach slices.

1 cup fresh orange juice
$^1/_2$ cup sugar
1 cup raspberries
1 cup peeled peach slices
2 tablespoons fresh lemon juice

In a small nonreactive saucepan, heat the orange juice and sugar, stirring, until the sugar dissolves, about 3 to 4 minutes.

Transfer the liquid to the bowl of a food processor and add the raspberries, peaches, and lemon juice. Process the mixture until it's liquefied. Strain through a sieve, pushing out all the juice and discarding the seeds.

Chill the puree until it is cold, then transfer to an ice cream maker and freeze according to the manufacturer's instructions. Transfer to a chilled bowl and freeze until firm enough to serve.

# A Fast and Easy Method for
# Sorbets and Ices

Don't have an ice cream maker? No sweat. You can make wonderful sorbets by *still-freezing* your concoctions, as opposed to *stir-freezing* them in an ice cream maker. Here's how.

Cool your liquid to room temperature, then pour it into a shallow casserole. Place the casserole in your freezer and let the mixture chill until it begins to ice heavily around the edges. Take it out and mix with a fork, breaking up the ice crystals. Repeat every 45 minutes or so, until your mixture is solid. Serve at any time, from slushy to solid.

An alternate method is to freeze your liquid to the solid state—overnight is best—without stirring it. When you're ready to serve, break the frozen liquid into pieces and put them in the bowl of a food processor. Process until the mixture has a texture somewhat like loosely packed snow, then serve or put it back in the freezer.

Bear in mind that different sorbets will have different textures; those with a high percentage of solids—ices made with fruit purees, for instance—will freeze more solidly than others. Sample as they freeze, to see how you enjoy them best. I love slushy ices myself, especially with chunks of fresh fruit on top. You may find, as I have, that you get a fuller flavor if the ice is not too hard.

If you find yourself making sorbets often, get in the habit of keeping little ramekins in the freezer to serve your ice in. Especially in the summer, you can use the few extra minutes a chilled bowl gives you to enjoy your sorbet before it melts.

# Chocolate Sorbet

This reminds me of a Fudgesicle, not thick and creamy like ice cream, but still chocolatey, cold, and refreshing. It's made with cocoa powder, sugar, and milk; some prefer the flavor of Dutch process cocoa, and that's fine if you can find it in your neighborhood. But I make it with Hershey's, too, and it tastes great. Serve with a splash of crème de cocoa, Amaretto, fresh sliced strawberries, or all by itself.

$^1/_2$ **cup unsweetened cocoa powder**
$^3/_4$ **cup sugar**
$^1/_2$ **cup water**
**2$^1/_2$ cups milk**
**1 teaspoon vanilla extract**

In a small saucepan, whisk together the cocoa powder and sugar. Add the water and whisk until smooth. Gradually heat the mixture, whisking often, for about 5 minutes, or until the sugar dissolves.

Remove from the heat and pour the liquid into a bowl. Blend in the milk and vanilla. Cover and refrigerate for 3 hours or overnight.

Pour the liquid into an ice cream freezer and freeze according to the manufacturer's instructions. Transfer the sorbet to a chilled bowl and freeze until hard enough to serve.

# Mango and Lime Sorbet

Here's a sweet, bright orange sorbet with a tropical twist of lime and mango. Serve it alone, or in chilled bowls with orange and pineapple sections. It's also great with vanilla ice cream.

1³/₄ cups water
³/₄ cup sugar
¹/₂ cup fresh orange juice
¹/₃ cup fresh lime juice
1 or 2 ripe mangoes

In a small saucepan, combine the water and sugar. Bring to a simmer, stirring occasionally, then simmer for 5 minutes. Pour into a bowl and cool to room temperature. Stir the orange and lime juices into the sugar water.

Peel the mango(es) and cut enough pulp from the pit to make 1 cup. Put the cup of pulp into the bowl of a food processor and process to a fine puree. Whisk the puree into the liquid. Cover and chill for at least 3 hours or overnight.

Pour the liquid into the freezer of an ice cream maker and freeze according to the manufacturer's instructions. Transfer the sorbet to a chilled bowl and freeze until hard enough to serve.

# *Wine Sorbet with Frozen Grapes*

*Makes 6 servings*

Pale pink rosé sorbet is served in chilled dishes, with a scattering of red and green grapes. It's a pretty, sweet celebration of the grape in pastel tones, just right after a light summer dinner on the patio or at the beach house. Freeze the grapes until they're rock-hard, but take them out of the freezer for 5 minutes before serving; you want them only semi-hard when you actually serve them. For a splash of color and fragrance, include a garnish of fresh mint, lemon thyme, or lemon balm.

2 cups rosé wine (may be sparkling rosé)
¹/₂ cup water
²/₃ cup sugar
¹/₃ cup fresh lemon juice
¹/₂ cup green grapes
¹/₂ cup red grapes

In a medium-size nonreactive saucepan, bring the wine, water, and sugar to a simmer, stirring occasionally. Simmer for 5 minutes, then pour the liquid into a bowl. Stir in the lemon juice and cool to room temperature. Chill for at least 2 hours. Chill a bowl to transfer the sorbet into.

Pour the liquid into the freezer of an ice cream maker and freeze according to the manufacturer's instructions. Remove from the ice cream freezer and transfer to the chilled bowl.

Halve the grapes lengthwise and spread them out on a plate. Cover with plastic wrap and freeze until hard. Chill as many small dessert dishes or ramekins as you will need.

A few minutes before serving, take the grapes out of the freezer. When they lose their rock-hardness, scoop the sorbet into the chilled dishes. Top with some of each of the grapes and serve right away.

# Grapefruit Rosewater Sorbet

*Makes about 1 quart*

I look for reasons to use rose water in my cooking, since Karen and our daughters love it so much. Here I blend it with fresh grapefruit juice to make a wonderfully refreshing and fragrant sorbet. For an elegant dessert, halve and section grapefruit and squeeze a number of sections into each chilled bowl. Add a scoop of sorbet, then garnish with slivers of fresh or candied rose petals.

**3 cups fresh grapefruit juice**
**$^2/_3$ cup sugar**
**$^1/_2$ teaspoon rose water**

In a small nonreactive saucepan, combine the grapefruit juice and sugar. Heat, stirring, until the sugar is dissolved, about 5 minutes, then transfer to a bowl and cool to room temperature. Cover and refrigerate or place in the freezer until cold. Chill a bowl for the sorbet to be transferred into.

Pour the liquid into an ice cream maker and add the rose water; don't be tempted to add extra rose water because it can overpower the flavor of the grapefruit. Freeze according to the manufacturer's instructions. Transfer the sorbet to the chilled bowl and freeze until firm enough to serve.

# Strawberry Mint Ice

*Makes about 1 quart*

Cool, refreshing, and deep red, this ice is infused with fresh mint leaves, forging a seasonal partnership my family and I love. If you don't have a source for fresh mint, use a mint tea bag instead; works like a charm. Serve small scoops of this alone, or with vanilla ice cream and fresh sliced strawberries on top.

1 cup water
$^1/_3$ cup sugar
$^1/_2$ cup loosely packed mint leaves, coarsely chopped, *or* 1
  mint tea bag
1 recipe chilled Fresh Strawberry Sauce (page 201)

In a small saucepan, bring the water and sugar to a boil, stirring occasionally. Reduce the heat and simmer for 5 minutes. Remove from the heat and stir in the mint leaves or tea bag. Let the mixture steep until cooled.

Strain the liquid then pour it into a bowl. Stir in the strawberry sauce then transfer the mixture to a glass or enameled loaf pan or casserole. Place the container in the freezer, covered with foil.

After about an hour, stir the mixture with a fork to loosen up any ice that's forming. Repeat this process a number of times, over the course of 3 to 5 hours. Check every 30 minutes or so, each time scraping the ice and pushing on it with a fork to break up big formations of ice crystals. Spoon the mixture into dessert bowls when it's firm enough to serve.

# Coffee Gelato

*Makes about 1$^1/_2$ pints*

Gelati are a kind of Italian ice cream, and though I've read they're generally less creamy than American ice cream, few recipes I've encountered in American cookbooks seem to agree. In any case, here is one favorite, with a texture somewhere between creamy, due to the egg yolks, and grainy, because of the brewed coffee. If you own a coffee grinder, you can add a classic touch by cleaning some of the fine coffee grounds out of it and adding them to the gelato; the finest grounds, I've noticed, collect in the lid of mine. Occasionally I like to add a tablespoon or two of coffee liqueur to this also. Enjoy the gelato just as it is, with Almond Biscotti (page 13), or in a sophisticated coffee sundae (see below).

$1^1/_2$ cups milk
$^3/_4$ cup sugar
4 egg yolks
1 cup strong brewed coffee
$^1/_4$ teaspoon vanilla extract
$^1/_2$ to 1 teaspoon very finely ground coffee beans (optional)

In a medium-size nonreactive saucepan, heat the milk and sugar, stirring, until the sugar melts, about 4 or 5 minutes.

In a mixing bowl, whisk the egg yolks and gradually whisk in the hot liquid about $^1/_4$ cup at a time. Pour the liquid back into the saucepan and cook over medium-low heat, stirring constantly, until the liquid reaches 180° on a candy thermometer. Pour the liquid into a bowl and cool to room temperature. Stir in the coffee, vanilla, and ground coffee beans. Cover and refrigerate for at least 2 hours.

When the liquid is well chilled, pour it into the freezer of an ice cream maker and freeze according to the manufacturer's instructions.

# Coffee Gelato Sundae

*Makes 4 servings*

Coffee Gelato is good so many different ways that I decided to combine all of them into this one extraspecial dessert. So we have a spoonful of mascarpone, a scoop of gelato, coffee liqueur, sliced banana, and chopped nuts. Sounds involved, but once the gelato is ready this can be thrown together in less than 5 minutes; you really don't even have to toast the nuts if you're pressed for time.

1 recipe Coffee Gelato (page 187)
4 ounces mascarpone cheese
1 tablespoon sugar

¼ cup coffee liqueur
2 medium-size just-ripe bananas
¼ cup chopped hazelnuts, walnuts, or almonds, preferably
toasted (page 20)

Prepare the gelato at least 3 hours ahead so it has time to harden in the freezer. Chill 4 individual ramekins or other small dessert bowls.

When you're ready to serve, in a small mixing bowl, mix the mascarpone and sugar just until smooth. Put a spoonful in each of the serving dishes. Put a scoop of gelato on top of the mascarpone, then cover each serving with a tablespoon of coffee liqueur.

Cut the bananas into small chunks and scatter some over the top of each serving, along with the chopped nuts. Serve right away.

# Fresh Mint Gelato

*Makes almost 1 quart*

Almost everyone grows mint, it seems, or has a friend whose patch of mint far outstrips the sum of its likely uses. In that spirit, I came up with this mint-infused gelato to celebrate one of summer's beloved fresh herbs. The exact character of the gelato will be determined by the mint you use; peppermint will yield a deep mint flavor, spearmint is milder, and orange mint will make a gelato with citrus overtones. If you grow lemon thyme, add several sprigs to the milk infusion for a pleasant lemony lift. To give this a hint of color credibility, I include a tablespoon of green crème de menthe, but that's optional if you think it's cheating. Serve alone, or with almost any chocolate cake, pie, or tart.

1½ cups loosely packed fresh mint leaves
2 cups milk
⅔ cup sugar
3 egg yolks
1 cup heavy cream
1 tablespoon green crème de menthe

In a medium-size nonreactive saucepan, combine the mint leaves, milk, and sugar. Heat gently, stirring, until the sugar dissolves (about 5 minutes) and the milk is hot to the touch. Cover, remove from the heat, and let steep for 30 minutes.

In a mixing bowl, whisk the egg yolks. Strain the mint milk and whisk it into the yolks. Pour the liquid back into the saucepan and cook over medium-low heat, stirring, for about 10 minutes, until it reaches 180° on a candy thermometer.

Pour the mixture into a bowl and cool to room temperature. Cover and chill for several hours or overnight.

Blend the cream and crème de menthe with the chilled liquid. Pour into the freezer of an ice cream maker and freeze according to the manufacturer's instructions.

# Banana Pineapple Sherbet

*Makes about 1 quart*

Do you know you can make sherbet in your food processor? Do you know you can do it very quickly, and it tastes wonderful too? Well, you're in for a pleasant surprise if you didn't. I tend to be Mr. Old-Fashioned when it comes to frozen desserts, so I was doubtful myself. But now I'm sold. The method couldn't be simpler: Just freeze slices of banana and crushed pineapple, then process with milk, maple syrup, and a drop of vanilla. This is a great way to make ice cream with kids, because there's no waiting. You just buzz and scoop!

> one 20-ounce can crushed pineapple in unsweetened
>   pineapple juice
> 3 medium-size slightly overripe bananas
> $1/4$ to $1/2$ cup milk
> $1/3$ cup maple syrup
> $1/4$ teaspoon vanilla extract

Drain some, but not all of the juice from the pineapple. Spoon enough of the pineapple into an ice cube tray to fill it—it should take most of the can—then freeze overnight.

About an hour before you make this, peel and slice the bananas into $1/2$-inch-thick rounds, and lay them on a small baking sheet. Freeze. About 20 minutes before you plan to make this, measure and chill the milk and maple syrup in separate containers. Refrigerate the processor blade and bowl.

If your food processor isn't a heavy-duty type, put half of the pineapple cubes into a plastic bag and smash them up a little with a hammer or rolling pin. Smashed or not, put half the pineapple and half the banana slices into the bowl of a food processor along with the maple syrup. Process on high speed for 10 seconds, adding half of the milk with the machine running. Stop the machine, add the vanilla, and push everything down into the bowl (it tends to ride up in my machine); continue to process until you have a smooth sherbet, adding more of the milk only if necessary to make it smooth. Serve at once.

Bag up the remaining fruit and use it next time.

*Variation:* Any number of fruit purees would work nicely here, in place of the crushed pineapple. Use your food processor to puree fresh, ripe, peeled mangoes, peaches, apricots, or nectarines. Strained raspberry or blackberry puree makes an excellent flavor base. And honey or sugar could replace the maple syrup; use honey at room temperature.

# White Chocolate Mint Semifreddo with Fresh Strawberries

*Makes 6 to 8 servings*

A semifreddo is a mousselike frozen dessert with a soft and creamy texture. It's often molded in a loaf pan, then cut and served, but it's simpler—and no less wonderful—eaten right out of a goblet, parfait glass, or custard cup. Here I like the combination of mint and strawberries, but you can vary this basic idea with other liqueurs; Amaretto is also very good. Incidentally, if you decide you like semifreddi, there are a number of excellent ones in Michelle Scicolone's good book *La Dolce Vita* (Morrow, 1993), the inspiration for this recipe.

$1/4$ cup white crème de menthe
9 ounces white chocolate, in pieces
1 cup very cold heavy cream
4 large eggs, at room temperature
$1/3$ cup sugar
1 pint ripe strawberries, sliced
fresh mint leaves for garnish (optional)

Put the crème de menthe and white chocolate in a bowl and place the bowl over a saucepan of very hot water; or use a double boiler. Melt the chocolate over very low heat, stirring occasionally to smooth. Remove the bowl from the heat and set aside.

In a large bowl, whip the cream until it holds medium-stiff peaks. Cover and refrigerate.

Using an electric mixer, beat the eggs and sugar on high speed for about 5 to 6 minutes, until light, fluffy, and quadrupled in volume. The eggs should hold a thick ribbon when the beater is lifted from the bowl. Gradually fold the melted chocolate into the beaten eggs. Fold half of the egg mixture into the whipped cream, until blended, then fold in the remaining egg mixture.

Divide the mixture evenly between serving glasses or custard cups. Cover them and freeze for at least 8 hours, removing the dishes from the freezer up to 20 minutes ahead so the texture has a chance to soften; but don't let it get too soft. When ready to serve, pass a bowl of sliced strawberries to go on top. Garnish with fresh mint if you like.

# White Chocolate Pecan Semifreddo

*Makes 8 servings*

Here's another white chocolate semifreddo I'm crazy about; my son Ben says this is like the best butter pecan ice cream in the world, only better, which pretty much sums up the sentiments of everyone who has tried it. In some ways, I find this semifreddo even more appealing than ice cream because it's so incredibly light in texture. If you want to serve a little something with this, a plain shortbread or nut cookie will do nicely.

## NUT MIXTURE

1 cup toasted pecan halves, cooled (page 20)
1 tablespoon sugar
2 teaspoons instant coffee powder
1/4 teaspoon ground cinnamon
3 ounces white chocolate, in pieces

SEMIFREDDO

7 ounces white chocolate, coarsely chopped
1 cup heavy cream
1¹/₂ tablespoons coffee or almond liqueur
4 large eggs, at room temperature
¹/₃ cup sugar

Put the cooled nuts, sugar, instant coffee, and cinnamon in a food processor. Grind briefly, until the nuts are coarsely chopped. Add the 3 ounces of white chocolate and process just until the chocolate is coarsely chopped. Set aside.

Put the 7 ounces of white chocolate in the top of a double boiler over very hot water. Stir occasionally over very low heat, until smooth and melted, about 5 to 8 minutes, then remove from the heat and set aside.

In a large bowl, whip the cream until it holds medium-firm peaks. Beat in the liqueur. Cover and refrigerate.

Using an electric mixer, beat the eggs and sugar on high speed for 4 to 6 minutes, until roughly quadrupled in volume. The beater should leave a thick ribbon behind when you lift it. Gradually fold the melted white chocolate into the beaten eggs. Fold half of the beaten eggs into the whipped cream, then fold in the rest of the eggs just until the mixture is evenly blended.

Fold half of the pecan mixture into the semifreddo. Divide the mixture evenly between serving glasses or big custard cups. Cover and freeze for 12 hours, removing the semifreddo from the freezer up to 20 minutes ahead so it has time to soften slightly. Pass the rest of the nut mixture when the semifreddo is served, to sprinkle on top.

# *Frozen Blackberry Yogurt*

*Makes almost 1 quart*

After a summer's worth of rich fruit ice creams, I'm ready for something a little leaner when blackberry season rolls around in mid- to late August. That's when I like to make this creamy plum-colored blackberry yogurt. It has all the body and much of the same appeal as a rich ice cream, but with a slimmer profile. The gorgeous, shocking color adds drama to summer dessert plates, so use it to jazz up plain fruit dishes, fruit compotes, pound cake, Amaretti (page 8), or Lemon Ice Cream (page 177).

2 pints fresh ripe blackberries
1 cup sugar
juice of 1 lemon
2 cups plain cold regular or low-fat yogurt

Put half each of the blackberries and sugar in the bowl of a food processor and puree until smooth. Strain the puree through a sieve, pressing firmly on the seeds to extract most of the juice. Repeat for the rest of the berries and sugar. Stir the lemon juice into the puree.

    Scrape the puree into a shallow casserole and refrigerate, covered, for 1 hour. Once the puree has chilled, blend it with the yogurt in a bowl and pour it into the freezer of an ice cream maker. Freeze according to the manufacturer's instructions.

# Frozen Peanut Cloud Pie with Warm Chocolate Sauce

*Makes 1 dozen servings*

    If you're a peanut butter lover, this will indeed send you off into the clouds! And, you'll love how easy it is to make. Everything is just whipped up in a mixer then spread in a peanut graham cracker crust. Freeze it overnight, then serve with warm 5-Minute Chocolate Sauce or store-bought; you could serve the pie alone, but it would be a downright shame to do this halfway, frankly.

1 recipe Peanut Crumb Crust (page 133)

FILLING

1 cup heavy cream
8 ounces cream cheese, softened
1 cup smooth natural salted peanut butter
$^3/_4$ cup granulated sugar
$^1/_2$ cup packed light brown sugar
$1^1/_2$ tablespoons vanilla extract

2 egg whites
$^1/_2$ cup finely chopped roasted salted peanuts
1 recipe 5-Minute Chocolate Sauce (page 198), warm, *or* 1
  jar store-bought chocolate sauce

Prepare the crust and press it into the bottom and halfway up the sides of an 8-inch springform pan. Bake for 10 minutes in a preheated 350° oven. Cool on a rack.

In a bowl, whip the cream by hand or electric mixer until it holds soft peaks. Cover and refrigerate.

Using an electric mixer, beat the cream cheese and peanut butter until smooth. Gradually beat in the sugars, then the vanilla extract; the mixture will be like clumpy cookie dough at this point, not fluffy. Thoroughly blend the whipped cream into the peanut butter mixture. Whip the egg whites until they hold firm peaks then fold them into the filling until smooth.

Scrape the filling into the crust and even it with a spoon. Sprinkle the chopped nuts over the pie and press them in lightly with your hands.

Cover the pie with foil and freeze overnight. Remove from the freezer 15 minutes before slicing. While you're waiting, prepare the sauce; if you're using store-bought sauce, warm it. Serve slices on their side, with a pool of sauce around each slice.

# Frozen Yogurt: The Straight Skinny

I wouldn't kid you on this: *Making* frozen yogurt is even easier than *buying* it! Prove it? Take 1 quart of your favorite flavored or fruited yogurt. Dump it in the ice cream freezer. Chill according to the manufacturer's instructions. How's that for easy?

Rather create your own custom flavors? Here are some general guidelines.

To make about a quart of any fruit yogurt, start with 3 cups plain (regular or low-fat) yogurt. In a food processor, make 1 to 1 1/2 cups fruit puree from fresh, canned, or frozen fruit. Sweeten the puree with 1/2 cup of sugar and process until smooth.

If the puree contains seeds, stir it into the plain yogurt with 1 teaspoon of lemon extract. Pour the mixture into an ice cream freezer and chill according to the manufacturer's instructions.

Plain creamy vanilla yogurt is an excellent partner for summer sorbets, pound cake, fresh sliced fruit, and berries. To make it better than the best store-bought, blend 1 quart of plain yogurt, 1 cup of heavy cream (light cream if you're watching calories), 3/4 cup of sugar, and 2 teaspoons of vanilla extract. Pour into an ice cream freezer and chill according to the manufacturer's instructions.

And if lemon is your flavor, prepare as for vanilla yogurt, increasing the sugar to 1 cup. Add 1/3 cup of lemon juice, the finely grated zest of half a lemon, and replace the vanilla extract with 1 teaspoon of lemon extract.

# The Finishing Touch:
# Sauces and Icings

Here is a short section dedicated to a few of the sauces and icings I use most often. Although my definition of a simple dessert is one that can generally stand alone, there are still those occasions when an icing is necessary, or a sauce offers a needed splash of color or textural balance; one example I can think of, which accomplishes both requirements, is the Raspberry Sauce (page 200) with Jim's Flourless Chocolate Cake (page 39). That's my kind of sauce because you can make it in under five minutes.

No matter what sauce you choose, remember that it should never upstage or drown out that which it accompanies; it should complement, not compete. How you apply a sauce also makes a statement about its place of importance in the overall scheme of things. Too much sauce, dumped right over the dessert, strikes me as uncivilized and in bad taste. The current practice of saucing the plate at the base of the dessert is a smart one, because the sauce doesn't intrude upon the visual integrity of a perfect slice of tart, or cake, or whatever. (On the other hand, if your dessert has a visual flaw, then by all means sauce it!)

If in doubt about whether your guests or family will prefer a sauce, serve it in small individual ramekins or a pretty communal serving bowl.

# 5-Minute Chocolate Sauce

I find a lot of chocolate sauce recipes unnecessarily involved. So I set out to come up with a basic sauce I could commit to memory, and flavor to suit the occasion; this is it. Use either semisweet chocolate, or good bittersweet chocolate if money is no object. In addition to the variations listed below, you can flavor this with 2 tablespoons of most any liqueur you prefer.

> ³/₄ **cup light cream**
> **8 ounces semisweet or bittersweet chocolate, coarsely**
>    **chopped**
> **2 tablespoons unsalted butter, cut into small pieces**

In a medium-size saucepan, warm the cream and chocolate over very low heat, stirring occasionally to smooth. When the chocolate is completely melted, 5 or 6 minutes, remove from the heat and whisk in the butter.

Mix in any of the optional flavorings listed below, and serve. Store the sauce in a clean, tightly covered jar. Reheat the sauce right in the jar, in a saucepan of hot water, with the lid loosened. Refrigerated, this will last for at least 2 weeks.

*Variations:* Chocolate Mint Sauce—Whisk 2 tablespoons white crème de menthe into the sauce with the butter.

Mocha Sauce—Heat the cream first, whisking in 2 tablespoons instant coffee powder. Add the chocolate and proceed as above. When the sauce comes off the heat, whisk in the butter and 2 tablespoons coffee liqueur.

# Crème Anglaise

*Makes about 3 cups*

Crème anglaise—vanilla custard sauce—is one of the most delicious, and certainly the most adaptable of dessert sauces: It goes with almost anything—warm pies and tarts, cobblers, crisps, and crepes—but doesn't interfere or compete with other flavors. Though it can be used warm, it has more body and better flavor if it has had a chance to chill first, preferably overnight. The key is not cooking the sauce too quickly, or letting the temperature exceed 185°—you risk curdling the sauce and you'll have to start over. I strongly recommend using a candy thermometer to gauge the temperature the first several times you make this.

6 large egg yolks
$^2/_3$ cup sugar
$2^1/_2$ cups milk
1 teaspoon vanilla extract

Using an electric mixer, beat the egg yolks with the sugar for 2 minutes, until it becomes thick and lemon colored. Set aside.

In a medium-size heavy saucepan, heat the milk until quite hot. Remove from the heat and pour into a large glass measuring cup. Gradually whisk the milk into the beaten eggs. Pour the custard back into the saucepan and cook on low to very low heat, stirring continuously for 8 to 10 minutes. When the custard coats the back of a spoon or reads 180° on a candy thermometer, remove it from the heat. Don't be tempted to speed the process by increasing the heat; the sauce will curdle.

Strain the custard into a bowl. Whisk in the vanilla and set aside to cool. Cover and refrigerate until needed. This will keep in the fridge for 3 days.

# Raspberry Sauce

*Makes about 1 cup*

Fruit sauces like this one are some of the simplest sauces to make, and they add a brilliant touch of color to your dessert plates. They're also light enough to cut through the richness of many desserts and deliver a distinct fruity flavor, which makes them very useful if you're watching calories. This sauce can be made with either fresh raspberries or frozen, thawed berries, and surprisingly it's difficult to tell the difference between the two. If you're using fresh berries, pick them over carefully and remove any badly blemished or moldy ones, because once you puree the berries the moldy taste will permeate the entire sauce. There are some easy ways to tailor this to your taste. If you want to add a little body, whisk in a tablespoon or two of raspberry preserves. Or add up to a tablespoon of framboise or Grand Marnier, a nice accent if you're using this with the mascarpone-stuffed peaches (page 164). You can't go wrong with this sauce.

> 1 pint fresh raspberries, *or* one 12-ounce bag frozen
>   raspberries, thawed and drained
> 2 to 3 tablespoons sugar
> juice of $1/2$ lemon or $1/2$ orange

In the bowl of a food processor, puree the raspberries and 2 tablespoons of the sugar. Pour the puree into a sieve placed over a bowl, and strain the seeds. Use a rubber spatula to push the puree against the sides of the sieve; it will take several minutes to do a thorough job.

Whisk the lemon or orange juice into the sauce, then taste. If it needs it, whisk in another tablespoon of sugar and any of the additions mentioned in the headnote. Cover and refrigerate until using.

# Fresh Strawberry Sauce

*Makes about 2 cups*

This is one of the simplest sauces I know, not to mention one of the most versatile, but you don't even want to think about making it until you've got your mitts on some good ripe local berries. You can serve this with crepes, on ice cream and pound cake, use it in trifles, as the basis for a wonderful strawberry ice (page 187), folded with melon balls for a quick compote, and—well, you get the idea. Add the sugar a tablespoon at a time, *after* you've pureed the berries; the amount varies according to the berries and personal taste. Even with perfect berries, this sauce can often use a squeeze of lemon juice, a splash of kirsch, framboise, or a drop or two of vanilla extract to add depth.

> 1 quart ripe strawberries, hulled and cleaned
> 2 to 4 tablespoons confectioners' sugar
> a few drops of lemon juice, *or* 1 tablespoon framboise or
>   kirsch (optional)

Put the strawberries in the bowl of a food processor and process to a fine puree, about 10 to 15 seconds. Pour the sauce into a bowl and whisk in the sugar, a tablespoon at a time, tasting the sauce after each addition until the flavor suits you.

If you think the sauce needs it, whisk in the lemon juice, framboise, or kirsch. Cover and refrigerate until using.

# Fresh Currant Sauce

*Makes about 1 1/2 cups*

Whenever we get the urge to move—generally after yet another protracted New Hampshire winter—I eventually come to my senses when I realize it would mean leaving behind my hidden patch of fresh currants up the road. Their season is short, and there have been years when the deer beat me to them, but for me, picking fresh currants is symbolic of everything I love about deep summer. Usually the pickings are rather slim, but when I have enough I like to make this sweet-tart sauce of fresh and

# Cooking with All Your Senses

Experienced cooks know that cooking involves all the senses. Cooking times are helpful, but more often than not they're simply a reference point, not the final word. Are the nuts sufficiently toasted? Are the perfect-looking strawberries in the market really ripe? Are the cookies done, the dough kneaded enough?

To really learn to cook, you have to open your eyes, sniff, poke, listen, and taste your way to success. I don't think this comes naturally to a lot of adults. Many of us are still haunted by voices from our youth telling us not to play with our food. But the best cooks, and the ones who have the most fun, are the ones who *love* to play with their food, for whom life in the kitchen is just one big adult mud pie in progress.

Whether you're making desserts, or dinner, or breakfast, make a conscious effort to tune in to your senses. Take note of things like textures, colors, and flavors; this is the raw data of the cook's occupation. Are the cookies always getting too dark before the insides are done? Is your pastry tough when the recipe says it should be tender? In order to measure your own results against any standard, you must be willing to process that sensory data in a critical manner. You also have to be willing to keep trying, adapting, and making subtle changes, even in the face of less-than-perfect results. Be patient with yourself, and don't expect overnight proficiency in the kitchen. Good cooking is the lifelong accretion of little lessons learned one at a time.

On a more practical note, start honing your cooking senses by looking for sensory clues when you read a recipe. Be on the lookout for how things should look, feel, taste, smell, and even sound at various stages, starting in the marketplace. Even if this information isn't given, you can make mental notes to yourself, or jot them in the margins of the recipe as a reminder; I find myself doing this frequently.

The days of learning to cook at our mother's or grandmother's side are all but history; today, most of us are self-taught cooks. But when you learn to involve all your senses, you won't feel alone in the kitchen.

cooked berries. The trick with currant sauce is to use just enough sugar to tame the acidity of the fruit, but not so much to mask it completely. That's the beauty of using fresh berries in the sauce in addition to the cooked, to keep the sour highlight of the fruit. We treat this like the treasure it is, using it sparingly on everything from home-made vanilla ice cream to crepes. If you can't find fresh currants—their season is mid-summer—check at a farmers' market, or ask your county extension agent to find out who grows them in your area.

1$^1$/$_2$ cups fresh red currants
juice of 1 orange
$^1$/$_3$ cup sugar
fresh lemon juice to taste (optional)

Put 1 cup of the currants into a small nonreactive saucepan with the orange juice and sugar. Heat, stirring, to dissolve the sugar. Bring the mixture to a boil, then boil for about 8 to 10 minutes, until the liquid in the pan is somewhat syrupy and just barely covers the currants; you'll have to pull the pan off the heat to stop the boiling and check it. If in doubt, better to have a little extra liquid in the sauce than too little.

Transfer the contents of the pan to a small bowl. Cool for 5 minutes, then stir in the remaining $^1$/$_2$ cup of currants. Cool the sauce to room temperature, then taste it; if it seems to need it, stir in some lemon juice.

Scrape the sauce into a jar and screw on the lid. Refrigerate. This will keep for a number of weeks in the fridge. Serve the sauce cold, at room temperature, or heated.

# Chocolate Sour Cream Ganache

*Makes about 2 cups*

I fall back on this easy icing all the time for chocolate cakes and tortes; you can't beat it for simplicity and good taste. The formula is just melted chocolate mixed with room-temperature sour cream; you could probably make it by instinct even if you didn't have the proportions. One of the pleasant qualities about a sour cream ganache is the slight sour tang, a good complement to the sweeter elements of a dessert. That said, there is room here for making this more or less intensely chocolate. These pro-portions yield what I consider an icing with just the right chocolate emphasis and proper tang. Taste it this way, then if you want, you can always fold an extra ounce of melted chocolate into the icing. The icing spreads best if it's had a chance to chill first, so it firms up a bit.

 1 pound sour cream, at room temperature
 8 ounces semisweet chocolate

Put the sour cream in a bowl. Melt the chocolate in another bowl set over a saucepan of hot water, stirring occasionally to smooth. Remove from the heat and cool the chocolate to body temperature.

Fold about half the melted chocolate into the sour cream. Add the rest of the chocolate and fold it in until the icing is uniform in color. Cover the icing and refrigerate.

After 45 to 60 minutes, the icing should have enough body to spread nicely. If you chill it longer than that, fine; just work it with a rubber spatula to smooth it out and limber it up.

# White Chocolate Sour Cream Ganache

*Makes about 1 1/2 cups*

There are many uses for this easily made ganache. I love a dab of it with almost any kind of crepe, or a dollop with pies, crisps, and cobblers. It makes an excellent icing, too, for many of your favorite cakes. And try some with fresh summer berries, garnished with chopped mint. Be sure your sour cream is at room temperature or this will not mix properly; if it's cold, the chocolate will stiffen before the ganache is evenly blended. Covered and refrigerated, this will last several days; stir briskly to make it smooth and creamy.

 6 ounces white chocolate
 1 cup sour cream, at room temperature

In the top of a double boiler placed over hot water, melt the white chocolate. When the chocolate has melted, after 5 to 8 minutes, take the insert off the heat and set on a rack. Stir the chocolate to smooth, then cool for 5 minutes.

Put the sour cream in a bowl and stir to smooth. Scrape the chocolate over the sour cream and stir until evenly blended. If you aren't using the icing right away, cool to room temperature. Cover and refrigerate.

# Cider Whiskey Sauce

*Makes about $^1/_2$ cup, 4 to 5 servings*

I like a sauce that I could make in my sleep if I had to, and this one qualifies: All you do is boil down cider and stir in whiskey or rum, and a little butter. Let cool and serve. One of my favorite fast desserts is just this sauce served over vanilla ice cream, with sautéed apple slices on the side. Cider Whiskey Sauce is also heavenly on apple brown betty, over warm baked apples, or on most anything with cranberries in it. Letting it cool to room temperature gives the sauce more body, but naturally you can use it right out of the pan if you like.

    2 cups fresh cider
    1 cinnamon stick (optional)
    2 to 3 tablespoons whiskey or rum
    2 tablespoons unsalted butter, in several pieces

In a 9- or 10-inch nonreactive skillet, bring the cider and cinnamon stick, if you're using it, to a boil. Once it reaches a boil, boil rapidly for about 8 to 10 minutes, until reduced to about $^1/_3$ cup; the liquid will cover the bottom of the pan in a thin layer.

Remove the pan from the heat and stir in the whiskey or rum. Stir in the butter until it melts, then scrape the sauce into a serving container. Serve warm or at room temperature. Cover and refrigerate leftovers.

# Index

orange and toasted coconut crème
brûlée, 83–84
sour cream raisin pie, 121–22

# D

dairyless orange tofu mousse, 86–87
dates:
    Medjool, with orange almond paste,
       168–69
drunken yeast cake, 60

# E

easy chocolate "crepe" for the kids,
    97–98
ethereal orange bread pudding, 73–74

# F

feta cheese, grapes, and basil, 163
fig(s):
    grape and, compote with bay leaf,
       148–49
    grape and, focaccia, 101–102
    hazelnut-crusted, with honey
       yogurt sauce, 167–68
    pie, 119
    strawberries and, in maple balsamic
       syrup, 142
focaccia:
    dough, 101–102
    grape and fig, 101–102
fool:
    blueberry lime, 88–89
    light chocolate raspberry, 89
Frangelico:
    chocolate hazelnut torte, 40–41
French sugar cake, 52–53

French vanilla bean ice cream, 171–72
fruit, 134–35. *See also* compote;
    specific fruits.
    brandied dried, and apple pie,
       115–16
    chunky summer, salsa, 144–45
    dried, in brandy, 166–67
    gratin, 160
    grilling, 153–56
    pecans, creamed blue cheese, and
       sliced fall, 162
    soups with yogurt, 154–55
    sweet ricotta and fresh, toasts, 100
fruitcake, dark chocolate, 47–49

# G

ganache:
    chocolate sour cream, 204–205
    white chocolate sour cream,
       205–206
garnishes, 138–39
gelato:
    coffee, 187–88
    coffee, sundae, 188–89
    fresh mint, 189–90
genoise, 61–62
ginger:
    blueberries and melon in blueberry,
       syrup, 146
    coffee-glazed gingerbread, 49–50
    custard, 82
    fresh berry compote in honey,
       cream, 136
    pear crostata with, preserves,
       127–28
    poached pear halves in, syrup,
       151–52
    Tess's whole wheat, cookies, 17–18
glazes:
    coffee, 49–50
    chocolate, 18–19

mocha chocolate, 37–38
strawberry, 112
golden shortcake biscuits, 63–64
graham cracker crust, 132–33
Grand Marnier:
chocolate pâte with raspberry sauce,
91
dried fruit in brandy, 166–67
drunken yeast cake, 60
strawberries Romanoff, 166
grape:
feta cheese, and basil, 163
and fig compote with bay leaf,
148–49
and fig focaccia, 101–102
wine sorbet with frozen, 185–86
grapefruit:
citrus and blueberry compote with
orange-flower water, 144
and raspberries in red wine syrup,
143
raspberry, and melon compote,
137
rosewater sorbet, 186
ruby red, and cranberry compote,
135
gratin of peaches and raspberries, 160
Greek honey and orange nut cookies,
11–13
grilled fruit, 153–56
bananas with peanut butter whipped
mousse, 156
butterscotch, pineapple slices, 157
peaches with warm blueberry sauce,
153–56

## H

hazelnut, 20–21
chocolate, torte, 40–41
coffee gelato sundae, 188–89
-crusted figs with honey yogurt
sauce, 167–68

maple mousse with toasted, 85–86
holiday dessert:
chocolate pâte with raspberry sauce,
91
honey:
dairyless orange tofu mousse, 86–87
fresh berry compote in, ginger
cream, 136
Greek, and orange nut cookies,
11–13
hazelnut-crusted figs with, yogurt
sauce, 167–68
-lemon syrup, 43–44
syrup, 11–13
honeydew melon, blueberries and, in
blueberry ginger syrup, 146

## I

ice cream, 170–71
chocolate and coconut-coated
pineapple, 158
chocolate stuffed peaches with
raspberry sauce, 164
French vanilla bean, 171–72
hardening, 175
how to make an, sandwich, 14
ice, keeping on hand for, 173
lemon, 177
maple rum, with pecan praline,
172–74
old-fashioned strawberry, 176
pumpkin, 177–78
strawberries Romanoff, 166
toasted almond, loaf with fresh
cherries, 178–79
toasted coconut mocha mud pie,
122–23
ices. *See also* gelato; semifreddo;
sherbets; sorbets.
hardening, 175
ice, keeping on hand for, 173

strawberry mint, 187
icing:
    chocolate sour cream ganache,
        204–205
    white chocolate sour cream
        ganache, 205–206
Indian pudding, maple, 78
instant desserts, 56–57

## J

Jim's flourless chocolate cake, 39–40

## K

kirsch:
    plum cobbler, 68–69
kuchen, peach and raspberry, 62
kugel, apple raisin, 76–77

## L

lemon:
    cake with wheat germ, 43–44
    cheesecake tartlets, 24–25
    creamy, tapioca pudding, 84
    honey-, syrup, 43–44
    ice cream, 177
lime:
    blueberry, fool, 88–89
    blueberry, sorbet, 180
    mango and, sorbet, 184–85

## M

macadamia nuts:
    triple chocolate chip nut cookies,
        15–16

mango and lime sorbet, 184–85
maple:
    cinnamon applesauce, 159
    Indian pudding, 78
    Mary's Shaker pudding, 74–75
    mousse with toasted hazelnuts,
        85–86
    oranges and pineapple in, rum
        sauce, 145–46
    rum ice cream with pecan praline,
        172–74
    strawberries and figs in, balsamic
        syrup, 142
Mary's Shaker pudding, 74–75
mascarpone cheese:
    biscotti tiramisu, 90
    coffee gelato sundae, 188–89
    creamy stuffed peaches with
        raspberry sauce, 164
    crepes, with cinnamon sugar, 95–96
    crostini of peaches, cider jelly, and,
        99
measuring, dry and by weight, 12
Medjool dates with orange almond
        paste, 168–69
melon:
    chilled strawberry, soup, 149–50
    raspberry, grapefruit, and, compote,
        137
mint:
    chunky summer fruit salsa, 144–45
    fresh gelato, 189–90
    strawberry, ice, 187
    strawberry wine soup with, cream,
        150–51
    white chocolate, semifreddo with
        fresh strawberries, 191–92
mocha. *See* coffee.
mousse:
    creamy sesame, 87
    dairyless orange tofu, 86–87
    frozen peanut butter, 94–98
    grilled bananas with peanut butter
        whipped, 156

# R

crepes, 94
French, bean ice cream, 171–72

## W

walnut:
    apple apricot strudel, 102–103
    banana crostata with, topping,
      129–31
    chocolate and, fudge tart, 124–25
    chocolate soufflé crepes, 96–97
    cider jelly, bars, 23
    coffee gelato sundae, 188–89
    couscous, raisin, and, pudding,
      75–76
    fig pie, 119
    the Greenery's oatmeal chocolate
      chip cookie, 9–10
    Mary's Shaker pudding, 74–75
    steamed black chocolate cake,
      50–51
    topping, 129–31
    triple chocolate chip nut cookies,
      15–16
    whole wheat pumpkin pound cake,
      44–46
    whole wheat, refrigerator cookies,
      7–8
warm berry shortcake à la mode,
    64–65
wheat germ, 6, 45

lemon cake with, 43–44
    pecan apple butter thumbprints, 6–7
whiskey, cider, sauce, 206
whole wheat:
    pumpkin pound cake, 44–46
    shortcakes, 64
    Tess's, ginger cookies, 17–18
    walnut refrigerator cookies, 7–8
wine:
    grapefruit and raspberries in red,
      syrup, 143
    grilled peaches with warm blueberry
      sauce, 153–56
    peach, blueberry, and basil
      compote, 140–41
    prunes stewed in port, 141–42
    sorbet with frozen grapes, 185–86
    sour cherries in port, syrup, 148
    strawberry, soup with mint cream,
      150–51

## Y

yogurt:
    cheese, 111–12
    frozen, 196
    frozen blackberry, 193–94
    hazelnut-crusted figs with honey,
      sauce, 167–68
    strawberry, pie, 111–12

# About the Author

KEN HAEDRICH is a self-taught cook who specializes in wholesome desserts and breads with character. Beyond producing delicious food, his mission is to simplify and demystify the cooking process so that even novices can bake with confidence.

Ken is a Julia Child Award winner whose previous books include *Country Baking, Home for the Holidays,* and *Country Breakfasts*. He lives with Karen Price and their four children on a mountainside in New Hampshire, where he bakes every day.